Winners

Crispus Attucks High School, Basketball, and Social Change

John Gipson and Stan Patton

Gipp Publications
Indianapolis, IN

ISBN: 978-1-943414-31-4

Production Credits:
Authors: John Gipson and Stan Patton
Editors: Laura Town and Rachael Mann
Publisher: Gipp Publications

CONTENTS

A Coach's Philosophy

Coach Ray Crowe always stressed to us the importance of discipline in his game plan and how carrying it out as he taught it would make us winners, not only on the basketball court but in the Game of Life. (Don't quit when things get tough.)

Being one of the fortunate few that made his teams left me with a feeling of blessedness that I can't explain. I only know that I accepted the limited role I had on the team and was thankful for the opportunity. Most of us on the team came from poor families, some worse off than others. Through it all, we came together as a cohesive unit and if one needed something, the fortunate other would come forward to assist whoever it was in need. We had talented underclassmen that were treated as equals because their performance on the court demanded it.

We never showboated or tried to show up our opposition as players. We just played out our hand to accomplish our goal in winning championships and consoled the other team after games. The fact that we did this shows me why we have lifelong friends from other teams today. Hub Hoagland, DDS, immediately comes to mind. I was always running into guys we played against back in high school and college downtown when I worked at the Canterbury Hotel in Indianapolis. We ended up talking so long our wives would have to remind us we had destinations or reservations to make. It was amazing to me that after fifty years guys could walk up to each other and remember names.

Wally Cox, the former Broad Ripple High School and Butler University star, came to a fiftieth anniversary celebration the Crispus Attucks Museum put on for the 1955 championship team. Bobby Plump is always around and was on a program honoring the 1955 team at Crispus Attucks Middle School.

Stan Patton, a teammate and former Indiana All-Star in 1956, said some lady recognized him in the Miami, Florida, airport. She was from Lafayette, Indiana, and was a Lafayette Jeff High School supporter. She talked so much about how good our 1956 team was that he almost missed his flight. It just goes on and on.

We were happy at how proud we made our families and friends during those glory days. The friends we made back then and now have been invaluable to us in many ways down through the years. A lot of these were of the Caucasian race and we are deeply appreciative of their genuine help and friendship.

By using basketball as a tool to get an education, most of us have been successful in life, some more than others. By applying Coach Ray Crowe's method of discipline, most of the guys went to college and fared well. Of the players as a whole, there are attorneys, firemen, supervisors, authors, insurance executives, a professional basketball player, businessmen, and countless other occupations enjoyed by the former Crispus Attucks players.

Only in Indiana is basketball so instrumental in paving the way for young men of all races to succeed socially, economically, and educationally while pursuing their place in life. I feel blessed to have played basketball with the "Big O" and all of my other teammates on championship teams back in high school.

I only wish Coach Crowe could have lived a while longer to see the teams he inspired and coached being inducted into the Indiana Basketball Hall of Fame. But, deep down, I think he knows. The Crispus Attucks players—especially the 1956 championship team—appreciated the Indiana Basketball Hall of Fame for its recognition of the team's excellence in its performance on the floor while displaying good sportsmanship. I can say Indiana teams today show good sportsmanship in playing the game, despite the current trend of showboating and trash talking all across the country.

I wish to express our gratitude to the pioneers of the Crispus Attucks High School dynasty. These are the late "Wee" Willie Gardner, an Indiana All-State player and former Harlem Globetrotter and New York Knicks star. Also, Indiana Mr. Basketball (1953) and Indiana University great and former Harlem Globetrotter Hallie Bryant. Last but not least, I commend the late Bailey Robertson, a Crispus Attucks All-State selection, Indiana Central College legend, and Harlem Globetrotter. All of these guys along with numerous others started the winning Crispus Attucks tradition. They are as much a part of Crispus Attucks's championships as the teams that won them. My special thanks and acknowledgment goes out to Oscar Robertson, my teammate and lifelong friend, who I deem the main (and only) reason for Attucks being good enough to be considered for induction into the Indiana Basketball Hall of Fame. He is the greatest all-around player to ever play the game, bar none.

—Excerpt from an article written by John Gipson for the induction of the Crispus Attucks 1956 undefeated championship team into the Indiana Basketball Hall of Fame

Dedication

To Ray Crowe (1951–1957) who, despite his stern disciplinarian ways, was a kind and good teacher who taught us how to deal with problems and obstacles throughout life through his coaching basketball at Crispus Attucks High School.

We definitely liked his philosophy of "NOBODY BEATS US." This kind of thinking helped him post the best win/loss percentage in Indiana high school basketball history! Coach Ray Province Crowe died quietly in his sleep at the age of 88 on December 20, 2003. This book is respectfully and reverently dedicated to his memory.

Coach Ray Crowe

Acknowledgements

This is a story of events and trials of Crispus Attucks High School basketball players **PATTON**, **GIPSON**, **BROWN**, **MILTON**, and **ENOCH** and how they became a part of Attucks's quest to win a state championship in Indiana. It touches on the racial prejudices that the school, coaches, and playing athletes constantly battled on and off the floor. Fortunately, their successes on the basketball court lifted many of these barriers, while instilling a sense of pride in the Black community.

This story tells of the success of Attucks, along with that of other Black teams, coaches, and players in the country. It shows the irony of how the paths of several players from Chicago and Indiana cross at each level of play down through the years. Others have written several stories about these historic accomplishments during the fifties and sixties, but none were written by any of the principals who actually competed.

We are indebted to those who granted interviews in the research of this book. They are Sam Milton, Joe Buckhalter, Bill Brown, George Smith, Jim Enoch, Henry Woods, Florence Scott, Oscar Robertson, and Bill Swatts.

Looking back over the years and trying to assess the whole picture, I have to give credit to those who helped and stood by us through the bad times as well as the good.

Robert Collins, sports reporter for *The Indianapolis Star*, was a staunch backer of Crispus Attucks basketball before the championships. He saw Coach Crowe put Gardner, Bryant, B. Robertson, and others through their paces when he was coaching the junior varsity team.

He watched them run the varsity into the ground on a daily basis. He smiled and said, "This is a champion in the making," predicting big things to come for Attucks in the future. Collins gave us superlative coverage. It made for good press, and we were put on the map. He appeared at many events and banquets that Attucks was part of and became good friends with several of the players, such as Bill Hampton, Hallie Bryant, B. Robertson, Oscar, and Willie Gardner. I guess this was a good story. Coach Crowe and Collins became close personal friends. We were all saddened at the time of his death several years ago. He is truly a friend that will be remembered and missed.

Joe Dezelan was a white coach who scheduled Crispus Attucks for games in basketball and football when all the other city schools refused. He was head coach of Cathedral High School, a Catholic all-male school. Mr. Dezelan was revered and respected by all in the Black community. When all the other city schools wanted to play us, he was always given first preference.

Bob King, an assistant coach at Shortridge High School in the city, used to scout for us during the tournament and after we got past the sectionals (city schools). When I look back, I can see how it was a tremendous help because we knew nothing about many of the schools in the state. He was appreciated and we let him know this.

All of our teachers and our principal, Russell A. Lane, have to be applauded because they made sure we were "student athletes." The public, last but not least, will never be forgotten because they lived and died with the Attucks team as they struggled through the hard times. They had to swallow all the bad calls and derogatory name-calling we had to endure. Fortunately, they got to see a championship.

Charley Maas, the late coach of Arsenal Technical High School, came to our rescue once when four buddies and I went to Tech H.S. to pick up some girls after school one day. The security guard wanted to lock us up for several bogus charges, but Coach Maas knew us and intervened. He knew that was not our style and he deadened the whole thing. He was a classy guy.

I believe God saw us as an entity to be used in bridging the gap between the races back then. It worked because all types of barriers were lifted and things began to get better over the years. We are truly thankful and blessed to have been a part of bringing about social change in the state of Indiana.

A special thanks to my wife, who is also my special friend, for her love, tolerance, and support down through the years. My son is also especially important to all my endeavors in life and, along with my wife, provides my sole reason and motivation for putting up the good fight in all of life's struggles.

About the Authors

John Gipson

In the spring of 1956, I had completed my high school education and athletic career at Crispus Attucks High School in Indianapolis, Indiana. It became Crispus Attucks Middle School in 1986 and a magnet high school in 2006. I stood six feet five inches at the time, but because I didn't have a particularly successful individual basketball career that matched the high goals I set for myself, most people thought of me as just another player who played at Crispus Attucks High School. After walking on at Indiana Central College and having a successful year on the varsity team as a freshman, I went on to develop into a good basketball player. I played on a city AAU championship team and Industrial League championship teams.

I also played on an all-star team composed of former Crispus Attucks players who competed against and defeated a college all-star team composed of college seniors who were standouts on their respective teams during the spring of 1959 at Butler Field House. We were led by the Fabulous "Big O," Oscar Robertson. Some of the outstanding college plyers were Herschel Turner of Shortridge High School and Nebraska University, Ron Loneski of Hammond Noll High School and Kansas University, and several others. I finished playing competitively in 1963 after three years of playing for Reece "Goose" Tatum of Harlem Globetrotters fame, on a team he formed after his Globetrotter playing days. Later, I got married, had a son, and worked for my father's cement contractor business part-time while working full-time for 32 years at Daimler Chrysler Motors. I retired in December 1998. I went on to work as a doorman at the Canterbury Hotel in Indianapolis, where I won the highest service award given in the hospitality industry, The Rose Award (2001). It's an acronym that means "Recognition of Service Excellence." I retired from the Canterbury in 2013. In 2012,

I worked on the Host Committee for Super Bowl XLVI, which took place in Indianapolis.

As mentioned earlier, the five of us have stayed in touch over the years, and later we got together to discuss and plan this piece of sports history. This tells of how and where we met and most of our trials and tribulations. We are all thankful, humble, and blessed to have traveled this long journey to be a part of sports history and bring social change in the state of Indiana. The Indiana Basketball Hall of Fame honored our accomplishments with the induction of the entire 1955 team in 2005 and the entire 1956 team in 2006.

Stan Patton

After graduating in 1956 and excelling on the basketball floor, Stan was selected for the Indiana All-Star Team as an alternate. He made the team as one of only three freshmen to do so on Tennessee State University's first National Championship team. But, by midseason, he was medically unable to play because of serious problems with his legs. He stayed for one year and returned home, working with my dad's cement business.

He gradually recovered and began playing again. He went up to Chicago to visit Buck Halter and play up there. He once played in a benefit game staged to benefit Bill Brown and Willie Gardner, and he dominated it. He scored about 28 points against a team consisting of former greats such as Bill Garret, former Indiana University All-American; Bailey League of North Carolina A&T; Sam Richardson; and others. He also dominated in a game in Chicago, raising the level of respect for Indianapolis players up there. He served in the Army for two years, came back to Indianapolis for a while, and then moved to Los Angeles, CA.

He became a Black Panther Party activist working for civil rights for Blacks on the economic and social fronts. His mom, Ms. Margie Patton, was our staunchest supporter. She raised three boys and one girl. We all loved her and she was always a loving, kind, and supportive person. Stan said, "I am proud of what we did and how proud we made our people in our accomplishments. My mother, who couldn't read or write, used to cut clippings out of the newspaper when my picture appeared in it, and left them on her employer's kitchen table for them to see. They would be amazed and glad for her to have a child doing something positive during those times. They had more respect for her after finding out these things. There wasn't a prouder person in the world."

****

I thank my friend and brother, Stan Patton, who helped research and write this book. Some of the research sources listed in the bibliography are *The Indianapolis Recorder*, *The Indianapolis Star*, the Indiana High School Athletic Association, Mr. George Smith of the National Collegiate Athletic Association Hall of Champions, and Mr. Ray P. Crowe—OUR THANKS TO THEM ALL.

Stan Patton, who provided vital information, data, and heart tugging personal accounts of his overcoming poverty said, "I am proud of what we did and how proud we made our people in our accomplishments."

I have said since our beginning at Crispus Attucks, what we accomplished was about giving our people something to cheer and be proud about. We didn't have much to feel that way about back then. I hope this book enlightens the young and the old of our historic accomplishments.

Chapter 1: The Beginning

My birthplace was Clarksdale, Mississippi. I was born on December 21, 1938. My mother, Pauline Nibbs, married John Gipson in 1937 in Clarksdale. My sister, Norma Gipson Stevenson, was born two years later. The first memories were of us leaving our maternal grandparents in Mound Bayou, Mississippi, and traveling to Chicago where we stayed with relatives for six months. Afterwards, we permanently relocated to Indianapolis where we made our home on the west side. My father worked as a cement finisher when work was available and my mother was a maid at the Severin Hotel until her early death at the age of 35 in 1951. I think it was from her that I got my niche of working in the public. After retiring from Chrysler after 32 years of employment, I worked as a doorman at the Canterbury Hotel in Indianapolis for many years, where I won The Rose Award in 2001. My father taught me the work ethic, always working somewhere and never expecting something for nothing.

I think these lessons have helped me through hard times of layoffs, strikes, and plant shutdowns over the years. Additionally, I cannot say enough about my two aunts who raised my sister and me. They were my mother's two sisters, Aunt Mary and Aunt Fannie. Aunt Fannie, interestingly, married my father's youngest brother. Aunt Mary, always the independent career type, married Prince Phillips. They had two children at the time my mother died. It was she who volunteered or was designated to care for us. She along with her family moved into our house on the corner of New York and Douglas Street on the west side of Indianapolis. She had become ill and wasn't one hundred percent anymore after suffering a cerebral hemorrhage. That's when my Aunt Fannie came in and assisted her with the care of my sister and I, and her family. She traveled back and forth from her house just down the street to our house to perform this noble task, not once complaining and always possessing a positive attitude. By the way, she had children of her own. These two aunts are truly loved and I can't say enough about them.

I always had a job of some sort, like shining shoes and setting pins at the bowling alley. This allowed me to sustain myself. I rarely went to my aunt or uncle for anything. My father also sent money to them for my sister and I. He traveled around the country working on construction jobs wherever available.

Chapter 2: Anna Anderson

My mother befriended an older lady who lived across the street from us, Ms. Anderson. Ms. Anderson had adult kids of her own. She knew my mother worked a lot of Sundays and we didn't go to church on these days. She asked if my sister and I could attend church at her church, Second Christian Church. My mother said yes, and we were picked up every Sunday and transported to church in a long car, sometimes also used for funeral services. This is where I met a lot of people whom I would become friends with and cross paths with later in my high school days. A few of my high school teachers attended Second Christian Church and I would certainly have encounters with them later in my high school days. One person stands out, though: Mrs. Nancy Powell, a history teacher.

I remember attending church one Sunday after we won our first state championship. Reverend Peoples called me up in front of the congregation to recognize me to all the member who didn't know me. Ms. Anderson was there, and later told me how proud she was of me in a "letter," which I still have all these years later. I realize it wasn't just an accident that I crossed paths with her during my life and I consider it a blessing because it contributed to the success I enjoy today in every aspect of life. She was truly special.

While attending Sunday school on Sundays, I met several people I developed friendships with throughout life. Some of these people were Walter and "Bibby" Blackburn, whose father, the late Cleo Blackburn, had established the Flanner House, a medical and social services center for the less fortunate. He was an icon in the community. Dr. Charleston Cox, a dentist who voluntarily gave his services in this program, became one of the most influential people in my life. I remember after I got married, I started up a janitorial company and went to him for a letter of reference.

When he got through, all who read it thought I was able to "walk on water." He was the best and gave me some valuable insight on dealing with life's ups and downs.

Chapter 3: Public School

I attended Public School No. 4 on the westside of Indianapolis. This is where I met several people who I am still friends with today. Maxine Stantley, Jesse Haynes, Cynthia Ford, and Beverly Douglas (deceased) are a few who come to mind. Maxine has always been like a sister to me and was a cheerleader at Attucks when I played. She was our class president and I was vice president.

When I was in seventh grade, my mother's youngest sister, Addie, a senior at Crispus Attucks, took me to a school program featuring Bob Jewell, a star on Attucks's basketball team. He was also the recipient of the Trester Award at the state tournament. It is the highest award given in Indiana high school basketball. It has since been named the Gimbel Award. When I saw him, I made up my mind I was going to play for Attucks someday.

Just being in the school was like being in a place of reverence. One year later I went to Attucks eighth grade to finish my grade school education. This is when I started seeing Attucks basketball players in the halls regularly. They were members of the first great team at Attucks in their senior year. Willie Gardner and Hallie Bryant (future Globetrotters) and Bailey Robertson (Oscar's older brother) were the stars and they were treated like royalty all over town. Bailey hit the last second shot that propelled them to a victory in the regional championship. I got to be real good friends with him when he was a senior and I was a freshman at Indiana Central College. He could shoot the lights out on a basketball court.

Willie was robbed of his senior year on the team when it was discovered he played a half season of freshman ball. Thus, his four years of eligibility were used up. It was a bitter pill to swallow, but he just continued on playing his senior year on the football team where he was chosen All-City.

Hallie was an All-Conference player his senior year at Indiana University and went on to play thirteen years for the Globetrotters. Willie was an All-Army selection while in the service, and then went on to star with the Globetrotters for three years. His contract was sold to the New York Knicks for $35,000, where he excelled during the exhibition season. He never got to play during the regular season because of an irregular heartbeat and had to retire. He was coach of the Ray Crowe All-Star Team composed of former Crispus Attucks players for two years and then gave up the sport all together.

He was the best big man to ever play at Attucks and was selected as one of the 50 greatest in Indiana. One day before he went to play professionally, he stopped by Military Park where I first started playing ball and encouraged me and told me to always play with better players, thus making myself a better player. I went to school the next day and told my friends I had shot around with him and no one believed me. I didn't care because I thought I had experienced something special.

John "Noon" Davis, Benny Cook, DeJuan Boyd, Charles West, Bob Jewell, Charles Cook, and "Tee" Toliver were all outstanding players in their own right. Boyd went on to Butler where he had an outstanding but brief stint with the Bulldogs basketball team. Noon Davis was selected All-Army while playing in special services during a tour of duty.

Chapter 4: The Senate Avenue YMCA

The YMCA, located on Senate Avenue, was the only place of its kind for the Black kids on the westside of Indianapolis to go for recreation. It offered a variety of activities to participate in, such as ping pong, checkers, chess, swimming, billiards, and basketball. I think just about every kid that went on to play sports in high school went to the "Y" at some period of time. I remember seeing a lot of the future Crispus Attucks players there when I attended during my younger years.

Mr. Benny Charleston, the brother of the Negro Baseball League great Oscar Charleston, ran the athletic program at the Y. Swimming was his forte, as he taught and coached the sport. The only drawback was there was no place to go to compete because the white swimming programs at that time had no desire to compete against Black swimmers. Mr. Charleston brought discipline, tough love, and a genuine concern for all the boys who participated in his program.

The Y was also a meeting place for a lot of local and nationally known civic leaders. The meetings were known as "Monster Meetings" and drew such prominent civil rights and political leaders as Booker T. Washington, Madame C.J. Walker, Walter White of the NAACP, and the local civic leaders, the Ransom family. The late attorney Willard Ransom's father spearheaded these meetings, which drew the icons of the city of Indianapolis at that time.

The YMCA was closed and later converted into a union hall. A new facility was constructed at Indiana Avenue and Blake Street. Mr. Charleston was once again in charge of the facility, which now had a weight room and regulation basketball floor. It opened in 1959 and was "the place to play." It had several industrial and church leagues that competed there. Bill Brown and I played for the now-defunct Kingan Meat Packing Company for which we worked. We won the first tournament played there. I scored forty points to set the gym record. Shortly after that, I think Bill Hampton broke it, scoring forty-five points.

While working at Kingan's, we met a lot of the people who had followed and supported us during our high school days. They were elated in meeting us and loved to talk to us about basketball and our experience while playing. Even the personnel office manager and his employers loved us. It was really humbling and nice to know people thought so well of us. They especially commented on our sportsmanship and humility. We were treated like royalty. It's something I'll never forget as long as I live. Most of them, by being older than us, are now deceased, but I still run into a few of them occasionally. The plant closed in 1968 and farmed out a few of its operations to Omaha, Nebraska, and the southwest states of the country.

After being laid off, Bill Brown and I went to the fire department and Chrysler, respectively.

Chapter 5: Tom Sleet—Grade School and Freshman Coach

Tom Sleet probably was the most influential person in the development and success of our contribution to the Crispus Attucks High School basketball program. Oscar related to us how Sleet used to give each individual on his teams' personal instruction on playing the game—things like setting picks, types of passes to throw, shot selection, etc. As I stated previously, he was the reason that I made the varsity at Attucks.

He was a two-sport star (basketball, football) at his Campbellsville, Kentucky, high school. He was supposedly an All-State selection there. He went on to star in football at Butler University in the late forties. He was enshrined in Butler's Athletic Hall of Fame in 1994 along with his mentor and our athletic director, Mr. Alonzo Watford.

Oscar attended the ceremonies in a show of his support for them. John Bridgeforth and I were pallbearers at Mr. Sleet's funeral in 1998. Oscar was a speaker at the funeral, eulogizing him, "He was a super guy, loved by us all, and sorely missed."

Prior to his death, Sam Milton and I went to visit him at St. Vincent Hospital. He didn't dwell on the state of his health, and only said that he didn't think he was going to be around long. His prime concern was how all the guys were doing. He was real upbeat and looking at him and talking to him, you never knew he was sick. He asked about Bill Brown and Jim Enoch and touched on different incidents involving all of us during our grade school years.

At our fortieth class reunion (Class of 1956), we presented his wife with a plaque commemorating our thanks and appreciation for all he had done for us. He was unable to attend and I'm sure he was proud that we appreciated his effort and time spent in prepping us for bigger things to come. He always said to everyone, "The 1956 team was my team."

Chapter 6:
Start of a Dynasty

In 1951, Ray Crowe, in his first year as coach at Crispus Attucks, took the team all the way to the state finals. He added his reserve team, which he coached while an assistant to Fitzhugh Lyons, with a few holdover seniors to mold a crack unit. Hallie Bryant, Bennie Cook, and John "Noon" Davis carried the team until midseason, at which time they picked up the incomparable Willie "Dill" Gardner. They withstood biased officiating to post an outstanding record that year. They played mostly small schools all over the state because of the refusal of most of the city schools to schedule them. After breezing through the Indianapolis sectional, they advanced to the regional final that they wone by "the shot," a last second basket by future superstar, Bailey "Flap" Robertson. With that heart-stopping victory, the Attucks fans were in a frenzy. Everyone had high expectations for the team to win it all.

The regional victory over the Anderson Indians by the score of 81–80 went into the history books as an all-time classic. They won the semi-state crown relatively easily. They then prepared for the state finals; that was to be no easy task. Willie Gardner fought valiantly, scoring eleven field goals during the game. John Davis fouled out, and that hurt the Tigers chances. They eventually succumbed to Evansville Reitz in the afternoon game. Bob Jewell won the Trester Award that night, a first for his school.

1951 Crispus Attucks Basketball Team

Front, left to right: Charles Tolliver, Charles Cook, Bailey Robertson, Hallie Bryant, Ben Cook

Back, left to right: Coach Ray Crowe, DeJuan Boyd, John Davis, Bob Jewell, Willie Gardner, Charles West, Assistant Coach Al Spurlock

Chapter 7: Years of Disappointments

1952

The next year, after making it all the way to the state finals, the Tigers had a splendid record, losing only to Lafayette Jeff in a Christmas holiday tourney and the Indianapolis sectional to eventual state runner-up, Arsenal Technical High School. The outstanding guard, Albert Northington, and the Mr. Basketball selection for the year, Joe Sexson, led Tech.

It was to be Willie Gardner's last season of play at Attucks due to a technicality. He was said to have played a half season on the freshman team, which they counted as a whole year. They counted it as part of his three-year limit of play in high school. It was a bitter pill to swallow; but he, being the strong person he was, went on to other things. It was a disappointing season overall, but everyone held their heads high and looked forward to the next year. Willie and Hallie were still selected All-State team members.

1953

The game that was taken away from Attucks two years before we won the championship was against Shelbyville High School in 1953 during the semi-state tourney. It was a hard-fought struggle the entire game. Attucks was down one point with seconds remaining when Hallie Bryant drove to the basket and scored. Two guys hacked him, and everyone just knew there would be a free throw along with the basket just scored. But, alas, they called a foul on Hallie and said he had charged the man. They disallowed the basket and awarded Shelbyville two free throws that sealed the game for them.

People all across the state were shocked and said it was a dark time for Indiana basketball. Bob Collins and other sports writers said it was an aberration. All the players were disheartened and the public was in disarray. This never deterred Coach Crowe as he prepared for the next season.

The game in which we got beat in 1955 was played at Connersville High School. There was a swimming pool in the basement directly under the floor, and the vapor from the water made the gym floor wet and slick. The referees didn't take this into consideration while calling the game. I'll bet we were called for traveling and carrying the ball twenty-five times that night. They were used to it, so they had a slight advantage, or you might say it leveled the playing field for them.

Willie Gardner once told me he had fouled out during a crucial game. As the game wound down, the referee called a foul on number thirteen. Willie, who was sitting on the bench, stood up and raised his hand. The crowd broke out into laughter. The one that really takes the cake was when at Attucks player was running down the floor beside an opposing player and the player tripped over his own feet. The referee whistled the Attucks player for a foul. We couldn't believe it.

John Bridgeforth was outstanding all year long in a reserve role for the Tigers. He got the crucial rebounds in the waning minutes of the game to allow Hallie a chance to win the game. He went on to star at Indiana State College.

The 1954 Season

After leaving grade school and having a good freshman season (12–3), we all made the reserve team, except for Oscar who made the varsity team. He was an instant hit on the varsity. Enoch was the best player of our group on the reserve team and even got to dress with the varsity after the reserve schedule was finished. Oscar and the 1954 team had a good year but lost to Milan, the small school that won the tournament that year. They even made a movie about it years later entitled *Hoosiers*. Bill Mason, who was selected to the All-Star Team that year, and Winford O'Neal were the senior leaders on that team with Oscar. Mason was the shooting guard and had a deadly one-hand push shot. He hit twelve straight shots in a semi-state loss that year. Winford O'Neal was the pivot man, and he had all kinds of spin moves and fakes around the basket. His career was cut short when he tore the ACL in his knee and had to undergo surgery. Many of us believe this team would have eventually won the state championship had Willie Merriweather and Winford not both gone down with injuries. Norman Crowe was the point guard and was a deadly jump shooter. He never turned the ball over during games. They only lost four games that year. Oscar led the team in scoring, and along with Bill Masson and Sheddrick Mitchell, kept Attucks in the thick of things all year long. Their record of twenty wins and four losses was right up there with the state's best.

Norman Crowe was always asked to guard the top scorer on the opposition's team. His quickness usually negated any offensive threat the opposing player tried. He was really out done once on a road trip to a little, small school out of town when Bill Mason jumped into the crowd chasing a loose ball. Some spectator he bumped up against told Bill, "Nigger, get up off me." Coach Crowe told him to just forget it because we were beating them pretty bad anyway. He still believes to this day they would have won the state championship if Merriweather and Winford O'Neal hadn't gone down with knee injuries.

After games, Bill Brown, Jim Enoch, and I used to go to dances at the Walker Casino Ballroom, which was located on the top floor of the Madame C.J. Walker Building.

Matthew Dickerson, who ran the dances, used to let us in free all the time. He was a big Attucks fan and used to announce us over the microphone when we came in after games. It was a great feeling.

We once got to hear The Counts sing there. They were former students at Attucks who went on to successful recording and stage careers. They were known nationwide and at one time had a number two hit on the rhythm and blues charts. One of The Counts, Robert Penick, used to play ball with me over at Military Park on the westside where we lived. They had recently gone back on the road doing "Oldies but Goodies' shows with other groups that they appeared with back in the early days.

Jamie Lee, who dropped out of high school in 1954 to go on the road with them, came back to Attucks two years later and graduated with my class, which was in June 1956.

I guess they are like wine, getting better with age. They lost one member of the group a few years ago, Robert Young, a baritone lead singer. The group sang at Willie Gardner's funeral. It was a very emotional time. Dill used to practice with them whenever he came back to town.

The year 1954 was a memorable one, graduating several musicians who went on to national acclaim in the music industry. Henry D. Cain (a pianist) recorded with the local group The Three Souls. Al Walton, who played several instruments, was a big hit with his group. James Spaulding, who played saxophone, played with some of the giants of the jazz scene. I almost forgot to mention that James Lee, of The Counts, played basketball at Attucks and was pretty good.

During the summers of 1953 and 1954, I used to play ball with some older guys in my neighborhood. They had pretty fair games, but never went out for the teams at Attucks as far as I know. We would get in one of their cars and go to different parks and outdoor courts at schools around the city. They followed us during our years at Attucks and were staunch supporters of ours throughout the years. They were Charles "Oogie" Powell, St. John Taylor, Eddie Matthews, and John Cunningham. We're still friends to this day. Robert Penick, of the nationally known singing group The Counts, was part of this group also.

Bernard McPeak—Referee

This man was the first Black referee in the state of Indiana. He started out, as I remember, doing grade school games. When we started playing freshman basketball, he refereed a couple of our games. He also was a football official during football season. This, I think, was his main thing.

I heard he was a football player in college in his time and a pretty good one. When he refereed our freshman football games, he used to practice punting the ball. He could punt it about sixty yards down field.

When we all graduated (1956), I heard he got to call junior varsity games. But I don't know if he ever got to move up as a varsity referee. It was tough even in the officiating capacity for Blacks back then. He was concerned about us in basketball games and would always let us know what we did wrong and why he had to make certain calls against us. I think this helped us out on the varsity level.

Chapter 8: Bill Brown

Bill Brown, who remains one of my closest friends today, was an outstanding all-around ball player from day one. He could handle the ball flawlessly, was strong inside offensively, and was the best rebounder pound-for-pound that I ever saw. He was strong and could get position on taller players, thus negating their superior height.

He started on the eighth grade championship team and the freshman team. He was the sixth man on the 1955 championship team and came in off the bench and won several close games for us. He was named second team All-City and All-State that year, and his performance off the bench prompted sports writers to coin the phrase "Fireman" (someone who comes in and puts out the fire).

He averaged twenty points per game and eighteen rebounds per game during our senior year in 1956. Naturally, he was an All-State selection and missed being on the All-Star Team that year, along with Oscar and Patton, due to a technicality. He went on to Tennessee State University, made the team, and would have challenged for a spot on the starting five had he not become ill that year. He had to drop off the team and come home after getting polio in his left leg. Coach McLendon saved his spot on the team in case he recovered because he was like no one he had ever seen before on the basketball floor. He underwent treatment and fought it until he eventually overcame it five years later. He is the only person I ever heard of coming back from being stricken by polio.

We used to go see him while he was in the hospital, and he was always in good spirits. After he left the hospital, he got around on crutches and never let the fact that he couldn't control his leg bother him. He went to parties, dances, and any place else we used to go. I believe his constant activity and nonstop moving around attributed to his recovery. Also, he always believed he would get better. I think all these things attest to his strong willpower and spiritual belief.

A few years later he was back on the basketball floor. He was one of a kind. When I used to practice against him during scrimmages and pick-up games, I used to do the best I could with him but he was too strong. I used to shake my head and pity all those guys on other teams we played who had to try and guard him. They really took a beating. He was always a low-key, nonaggressive person off the basketball court, and it took a lot for him to lose his composure. I guess knowing he would handle most people in a fight or confrontation contributed to his self-assuredness. He was really one of a kind. His mom, Ms. Berneice Brown (deceased) was a sweetheart and always treated us like we were her own. She was one of the few mothers that actually came to see our games. I remember once when I was going out of a game and on my way to the bench, I saw her standing near our bench and she said, "Way to go, 'Big Gipp.'" She, along with being proud of her son, was glad to see me do well also.

That is why she was always special to me. Once, during the 1980s, Brown, Sam Milton, Bill Scott, and myself (Gipson) attended the unveiling of a statue honoring Oscar at the Indiana Basketball Hall of Fame in New Castle, Indiana. When Oscar gave thanks and addressed the audience, he paid Bill the supreme compliment. He said, "When we used to play in high school back in 1956, one of my teammates always went up against taller players every night. He always came out on top. He is Bill Brown."

Brown was really touched to be mentioned at a ceremony for Oscar by Oscar. This shows the class act that the "Big O" is.

Sam Milton

Sam came up to Indianapolis from the south while in grade school. When he got here, they put him back a grade, something they always did to Black kids back then. He went to Public School No. 17 and Attucks eighth grade, where he was a star on the basketball team. He was tall as a young kid, about six feet tall, which was why he started out playing the center position. He was a good rebounder and had great fade away jump shots and a nice hook shot. He hit the winning basket during the championship game against Public School No. 26. He grew only an inch in high school, and that was when he switched to playing a guard position. He could handle the ball well, and his great jump shot and quickness is what made him a fixture in Attucks future basketball plans. He didn't play much after graduating and married and settled down with his high school sweetheart, Carol Clark. They had one son, Sammy Jr., who went to college at Vincennes Junior College and challenged for a spot on the basketball team. Sam remains our good friend to this day.

Jim Enoch

Jim came here from the south as a child and went to Public School No. 5, where he started playing basketball. He was tall and able to shoot with either hand. He went on to Attucks eighth grade where he was a starter on the team, playing forward and center.

He played on the freshman team with us and was a starter. He was a starter on the reserve team, often leading the team in scoring. He did so well, he was moved up to varsity when the reserve team finished its schedule. He dressed in the remainder of games and played in some of them.

He, like all of us, played more than one position on the team. This is why we had such a great team in 1956, something I didn't realize until later years. After graduating in 1956, he matriculated to Clark College in Atlanta, Georgia. He was a star on the varsity as a freshman. After a brief marriage, he moved to St. Louis, Missouri, where he worked for McDonnell Douglas Aircraft Company until his retirement. He has one daughter, Helen, who graduated from IUPUI in Indianapolis. He told me once while discussing our playing careers, "We were treated by royalty by the fans."

Bill Brown and Oscar Robertson attended Public School No. 17 and Crispus Attucks eighth grade. This was the same path several of the older Attucks stars took on their way to Crispus Attucks. Willie Gardner, Bailey Robertson, John Davis, Benny Cook, Hallie Bryant, and Cleveland Harp, along with Bill Mason and Winford O'Neal, attended these schools.

Jim Enoch attended Public School No. 5 and Attucks eighth grade. I attended Public School No. 4 and Attucks eighth grade. Stan Patton attended Public School No. 87.

Thus, we all met and started out on our quest to make the varsity at Crispus Attucks High School. None of us knew, or even thought about how, things would turn out for us in the end. It couldn't have turned out better, and I guess we were destined to be part of sports history in the state of Indiana.

Chapter 9: Crispus Attucks Basketball Practice

When coach had basketball practices, the first thing was warming up. We would run about fifty laps around the gym first. The reason for so many was the fact that our gym was small and not regulation size. We would then take a breather to wind down, and then go into our drills. We would practice defensive drills such as sliding from side to side while striving to move booth feet at all times. The next drill was pivoting on each foot interchangeably. Following that would be dribbling a basketball around chairs, alternating hands in the process. The forwards and centers would practice tipping the ball to the basket repeatedly and then finally tipping it in. This was to keep the ball alive in a game situation. We would then do figure eight drills with three men moving the ball up the floor in a fast break situation.

We would then practice our offensive plays, which consisted of out-of-bounds plays (inbounding the ball), set plays involving players on either side of the floor, and plays that started with the ball going inside to the center or starting with it going to the forward in a pick-and-roll sequence. Last of all, we would practice a zone defense and shoot free throws.

Coach would then have the starters scrimmage against the subs for about an hour. We would then run about fifty laps, shower, and go home. He said not being in shape was the downfall of his first good team in the state finals in 1951, and he vowed it would never happen again. That's why we could run full speed the entire game.

Homeroom

All varsity players were in a study period monitored by coach to assure everyone was keeping up with his studies and attending classes. This was called being in homeroom. He would be able to give assistance to anyone who needed it, especially in mathematics, which he taught. It was a good thing, and I think all of us benefitted from it.

Chapter 10: The Pinnacle of Success—The '55 Season

Willie Merriweather, our All-State forward on the 1955 state championship team, set a single season record for shooting percentage that still stands today. He shot .707 from the field, which is hard to believe. Once, during the sectional in 1955, Bill Hampton hit eight straight shots in a low scoring game. The other team stalled the ball most of the game to keep the score down. They also played a zone defense to prevent the ball from going inside to the pivot. Hampton ripped the zone to pieces with his deadly jump shot from the corner.

During the regional in 1955, my buddy Sam Milton hit sixteen points in the fourth quarter. He was on fire and he came in off the bench. He made the All-Regional team.

Sheddrick Mitchell, our center in 1955, was sort of the unsung hero. He was steady, consistent, and averaged about seventeen points per game and 10 rebounds per game. During the championship game against Gary Roosevelt, he contributed eighteen points and about nine rebounds. Our entire first string made First Team All-State along with Bill Brown, who made the second team.

Bill Scott, our point guard, was his steady self, hitting the open man, driving the ball to the hoop, and, along with Bill Hampton, dominating defensively. We had an awesome team. I can just simply say about Oscar, he was the best all-around player to play the game. He was like a coach on the floor and always, always got everyone involved in the game.

The most memorable and exciting game I remember that years was when we played Shortridge High School in the championship game of the Indianapolis City Tourney. It went into sudden death, which meant the first team that scored won the game. Oscar jumped center on the jump ball, got the tip, and after receiving the ball back waved the other starters to the side of the floor. Naturally, their defensive men went with them. Oscar dribbled to his right, faked his man as if he was going to drive on him, and raised up for the game winning shot. It was nothing but net and brought the house down because no one had ever seen anything like it done before. He was now a legend in the basketball history of Indiana. One of my friends was on that Shortridge team. His name was Herschell Turner, who was an all-around athlete at Shortridge, running track and playing basketball and football.

The Final Game

In the championship game of 1955, we jumped out to an early lead, which we never relinquished. It was about eight to nine points difference most of the first quarter. Oscar was distributing the ball in so as to get all our starters into the flow of the game. Whenever Gary Roosevelt would hit a couple of shots, Oscar would go on an offensive binge, hitting two or three shots in a row to maintain our lead.

Willie Merriweather was doing his thing on the offensive boards and getting Dick Barnett to foul him. He didn't hit many baskets during the game, but he was deadly from the foul line.

Jake Eison and Dick Barnett carried Gary Roosevelt all game long, but they weren't enough for our team, which was ten men deep. Anybody who went in could hurt you.

Bill Hampton and Bill Scott did a superb job defensively on their guards the entire game. They couldn't get many shots and this hampered their team's effort. Sheddrick Mitchell was outstanding on the boards and also had a good game offensively, scoring eighteen points. Our subs came in and didn't miss a beat. Brown scored eight points, Stan Patton scored four, and I also hit two straight baskets in the last quarter. The final score was 97–74.

The newspapers said it was our "coronation" and we were crowned "kings." It was a historic night and one that is still remembered to this day.

Oscar could have set a new state final scoring record, but on the last play of the game he opted to pass the ball to Willie Burnley, one of our subs that hadn't scored during the game. As a result of not shooting himself, Wilson Eison of Gary outscored him by one point and set the record. This attests to his greatness on the playing floor.

Oscar Robertson

While in high school during my junior and senior years, I used to work in the Visual Aids Department. It was run by one of the teachers, Ms. Ethyl Kuykendall. She was nice and offered me the job one day out of the blue. I jumped at the opportunity because I could perform my duties during school hours. She always scheduled me whenever I had free periods. It was a godsend for me because I couldn't work during basketball season because of practice after school. I got paid once a month and was able to pretty much take care of any expenses I had, such as lunch money, haircuts, schoolbook rental, etc. When basketball season was over, we all would go to the golf course and caddy.

Brown, Enoch, and I would usually go to Meridian Hills, and Patton would go to Broadmoor Country Club. The club members we would caddy for were glad to tell other members that we were good caddies. Wayne Timberman and his son, Wayne Jr., were nice to us and made sure we got out whenever we wanted. Once, when all the caddy slots had been filled, Wayne Jr. let me help him clean golf clubs so I could make some money and not go home empty handed. When golf season was over, I would set pins at the bowling alley. I always found something to do. I never had to depend on my aunt for anything that I wanted.

Crispus Attucks High School, Indianapolis, Indiana. The first all-Black high school basketball team to win a state championship in the history of American sports. 30–1 record.

Front row: Stanford Patton, Sam Milton, William Hampton, William Brown, William Scott, Johnny Mack Brown

Back row: Coach Ray Crowe, Willie Merriweather, John Gipson, Sam Clemons, Sheddrick Mitchell, Willie Burnley

Crispus Attucks High School

Indiana Basketball Firsts

- ***1st*** all-Black high school to win a state championship in American sports (nonsegregated)
- ***1st*** Indianapolis school to win an Indiana State Tournament
- ***1st*** undefeated team to win the Indiana State Tournament
- ***1st*** state champion to have its starting five named First-Team All-State selections
- ***1st*** Indianapolis team (and only) selected as one of the Top Ten Sports Stories of the Twentieth Century in Indiana sports history
- ***1st*** Indianapolis team to be inducted into the Indiana Basketball Hall of Fame
- ***1st*** school in Indiana basketball history to be inducted into the Indiana Basketball Hall of Fame two times (2005 and 2006)
- ***Only*** Indianapolis team to win seven consecutive regional titles
- Crispus Attucks coach Ray Crowe has the best winning percentage in Indiana basketball history with a record of 179 wins, 20 losses

Chapter 11: Crispus Attucks Cheerleaders

The cheering squad at Crispus Attucks was one of the best in the state. Ms. Mary Oglesby headed it. She had standards that had to be met to get on the squad. They had to be of good character, dress tastefully, and be outgoing. The girls on the squad during our championship days were Maxine Stantley, Glendonia Smith, JoAnn Buckner, Charlotte Clark, and Stella Barker in 1955. The squad in 1956 was made up of Maxine, Stella, Sandra Minter, Cynthia Ford, and Dorothy Simmons. Carolyn Edwards, Dolores Webster, and Barbara Broadus headed the 1951 squad up. Barbara Crowdus, Herbert Jackson, Jesse Canady, and Marilyn Smith were in 1953. In 1954, there was Herbert Jackson, Alicia Smith, Delores Campbell, Imogene Thompson, and JoAnn Buckner.

Edwina Bell Edelen cheered in 1942–1946 and wrote the infamous "Crazy Song." Maxine Stantley Coleman continued her promotion and support of Crispus Attucks High School for many years by heading the 1956 Class Reunion Committee. She put out a newsletter and supervised the scholarship committee that gave out a scholarship each year to worthy students who were siblings of Attucks graduates and any others who were worthy. They all were a source of support to the athletic teams back then, especially at games out of town.

Crazy Song

O, Shortridge was rough,
O, Shortridge was tough.
They would beat everybody,
But they can't beat us.
Hi-de, hi-de, hi-de, hi,

Hi-de, hi-de, hi-de, ho,
That's the skip, Bob, beat-um.
That's the crazy song.
O, they'd score some points,
Right over the line.
But we never did mind,
They were so far behind.

By: Edwina Bell Edelen

Chapter 12: The Dream Season

On November 19, 1955, *The Indianapolis Recorder* ran a news article stating that the use of Butler Fieldhouse was no longer available to Crispus Attucks for its home games. "Butler Cutting Fieldhouse Floor Out from Under 'Gymless Wonders'" was the headline in the paper. That meant the first home game, which was to be played November 20, was to be switched to the floor of Arsenal Technical High School (Tech). As Tech only seated 4,500, the game was an instant sell out. Attucks received 1,000 tickets for its student body, and the remaining 3,500 tickets were split between Terre Haute Gerstmeyer and the public.

Dr. Maurice O. Ross, president of Butler University at that time, stated that although everyone was critical of Attucks use of the floor, it had no influence on him denying the Tigers use of the floor. He claimed that he tried to accommodate other city schools as well and couldn't honor some dates that Attucks asked for. L.V. Phillips tiptoed around the situation, saying the Indiana High School Athletic Association (IHSAA) tried to defend Attucks from criticism in that respect because he and his group, the IHSAA, were sympathetic to its problem. He finalized his statement by saying he hoped Indianapolis would build Attucks a gym because they deserved it. Many thought L.V. Phillips, who was the commissioner of the IHSAA, didn't handle the situation well. It didn't matter; Attucks went undefeated anyway (31–0).

After relishing winning the championship in 1955, the returnees (myself, Patton, Brown, Milton, and Oscar), started focusing on winning another one our senior year. When basketball season rolled around, expectations for us were high. Oscar again was the catalyst in our pursuit of another championship. He, along with Bill Brown, Stan Patton, Sam Milton, and myself, composed the starting five.

Crowe brought up Al Maxey from the reserve team and also added sophomores Ed Searcy, Levern Benson, Odell Donell, and Jim Enoch and seniors Buzzy Swanigan and Henry Robertson. Henry was Oscar's middle brother and was a good all-around athlete, and was excellent in track and football as well as basketball.

Members of the 1955 and 1956 Championship Teams

Left to right: Stanford Patton, Bill Brown, Sam Milton, John Gipson, Oscar Robertson

Everyone was pretty even in talent, with only experience being the difference between the seniors and underclassmen. We dominated basketball in the state once again, winning the city tournament and the state title again. We did the unthinkable by going undefeated in thirty-one games. Halfway through the season, Crowe was looking ahead to the next year, knowing he had to get the underclassmen ready because he realized Oscar would not be back. He informed be I would be coming off the bench and Ed Searcy would be starting in my spot. Sam Milton also gave way to Al Maxey, a tremendous defensive player at the guard position. I was disappointed, but I was thankful to be a part of the team and I told Coach Crowe this, accepting the change. I didn't consider it a demotion because I still played a lot. I graduated midyear (January), so I was not included in the tournament. Everything went well, and we five maintained our close relationship through the remainder of the school year and up to the present time.

We get together whenever Patton and Enoch come into town. Patton resides in Miami, Florida, and Enoch in St. Louis, Missouri. Sam Milton survived prostate cancer, and I was there for him during his surgery and convalescence. He, in turn, did the same for me when I had both knees replaced, taking me to rehab, etc.

When Brown had to drop out of Tennessee State College, we would go by and pick him up as if he never was sick. He overcame his bout with polio and showed no sign he ever had it. Jim Enoch constantly calls, checking on me and my wife, who suffers with arthritis. All these four guys are truly my brothers. Our team was awesome and beat all of our opposition by an average score of fifteen points or more. We had a record of 31–0. Any doubts as to whether we could measure up to the team of the previous year were dismissed.

Once during a game in the state tournament (1956), Oscar fouled out and everyone thought we were lost without him. Brown and Patton, while going back on the floor to continue the game, said, "Let's show them we aren't a one-man team." Brown proceeded to set a rebounding record (most rebounds in a state final) that still stands today. Patton took the team on his back in the fourth quarter and we never missed a beat. He scored nineteen points that game. Everyone found out Attucks was a team, not a one-man show, although our one man was the best to ever lace up some sneakers.

There were only four teams that I saw play over the years that might match up with our 1956 championship team. They were Washington, Ben Davis, the Pike team of 2003, and a team from Marion, Indiana.

The game I contributed to most was against Tech during the final game of the city tournament. Patton was out with an ankle sprain and Bill Brown was out in foul trouble. We were down 12–2 at the end of the first quarter. I went in and picked up the rebounding, blocked several shots, and we caught up to go in at halftime in the lead. We never looked back and won the city tournament for the second straight year.

Oscar, Brown, Patton, and Maxey all made the First-Team All-Tournament Team. Our championship team of 1956 is the measuring stick by which teams are measured by today as far as ability, talent, and cohesiveness go.

Henry "Cookie" Woods, who played for Tech High School in 1956 and 1957, was a real good friend of mine and still is. We talk occasionally when we run into each other at reunions and on the streets. He paid us the supreme compliment, saying, "I loved playing against you guys. Although I knew you would beat us, one thing I can say is that you all were always gentleman on and off the basketball court."

Edward "Easy Ed" Hurt, who starred for the Shortridge High School Blue Devils, and I were having a beer one night at the Masterpiece Night Club. He told me something I had never really given much thought about. He said, "You guys beat us six times in two years, three times in 1955 and three times in 1956. That's something that is unheard of." He thought they should have won at least one or two games. He just couldn't comprehend it. Stan Patton said, "Once when we had beaten someone in the regional, one of the opposing players was crying after the game. His father went to him and told him crying wasn't going to help anything. He told him to go over and shake our hands and be glad to have played against us because, 'Nobody is going to beat them. They're too good.'"

Once Patton faked a guy so pretty, the referee came up to him and said, "That sure was a hell of a move you put on that guy." During the whole time we played, no opposing player ever called us out of our name or used any kind of slurs toward us. They always had the utmost respect for us and shook our hands afterward.

Our biggest problems were the referees and some of the white fans or public. The thing most disturbing was not being able to stop anywhere and eat in the restaurants in the towns we played in or Indianapolis. If it was a short road trip, we usually came on back home without stopping anywhere.

At games, I recall all the white fans sitting on one side of the fieldhouse and all the Blacks on the other side. It was always quiet on their side because we were usually so far ahead in the score they had nothing to cheer about. They just sat and watched our precision machine in action. Many times on road trips to away games we couldn't stop at restaurants or cafés to eat or use the restroom. We ate after the games at places contacted weeks before our games by our athletic director, Lon Watford. He would drive to the small town or city where we were to play and go to the restaurants until he found one that would take us. Ninety-five percent of the places wouldn't serve Blacks during the fifties. Most of the towns didn't have any Black citizens, and the ones that did had only a few. These few usually fared well because everyone knew them and they pretty well stayed in their place. We always won the games we played, and all the townspeople would show up at all the games.

They would crowd around the front of the restaurant hoping to get a glimpse of us, curious to see if all the stories they had heard about us were true. They rarely did because we were always served in the back banquet room. When we boarded the bus for home, they would be all around as far as you could see. There were never any incidents that I can recall, but racial epithets were hollered out sometimes.

We always displayed good sportsmanship and carried ourselves like gentlemen. But on the floor, we gave no ground until the final horn sounded. We played a pressing defense the whole game, while fast breaking nonstop. Our coach didn't like any "soft" players and wouldn't tolerate us giving in to anyone.

We weren't allowed to question the referees at any time; if we did, we were benched. Our only recourse was to stick to our philosophy or game plan, if you wish, and that was to jump out to a fifteen- or twenty-point lead and never let up. This way we took the referees out of the game. Usually, the opposing team had nothing but admiration and respect for us when the game was over. They were amazed of the things we did on the court. We couldn't dunk the ball back then during the games. If you did, they would disallow the basket and place a technical foul on you. They even disallowed dunking during the warm ups. They said it demoralized the opposition.

I remember one time when we beat a team in Michigan City, Indiana, by 75 points (125–53). We had seven players in double figures. My buddy Bill Brown had twenty-two points and twenty rebounds. The Big O, as usual, led the way in scoring and assists. I scored thirteen points and had eleven rebounds.

We won all of our games in 1956 by an average margin of fifteen points and went undefeated. It was the first time in the history of the tournament this feat had been accomplished. The one thing that really hurt was the team not being allowed to take the victorious ride on the fire truck around Monument Circle. The Big O still can't forgive them, and I concur.

After the game's ceremonies and trophy presentation, we went back to the locker room where Coach Crowe had us all join hands and say the Lord's Prayer. He thereafter congratulated us and warned us of our being under a microscope from that day on. We had to be on our best behavior at all times. We all compared the gold rings we received and relished our triumph.

We showered, left the fieldhouse, and went outside where fans were waiting for us. After greeting everyone, it was announced that a bonfire celebration would be held at Northwestern Park. We got on a fire truck provided by the city and proceeded there, thinking we would go downtown and around the Circle, which we never did. It's something we think about to this day.

Championship Parade, 1955

Most of us couldn't really comprehend what we had accomplished those two fabled years. I guess when you're young you don't dwell on those things. The most amazing thing about the whole thing is we didn't have a gym to play in. I guess you could say we were a "road team." Our success was largely due, I think, to the coach having us in tip-top shape at all times and the approach he had us take in our quest for excellence on the basketball court. On and off the court, we never taunted any of our friends or opposition, and I think that's why we are still friends with them to this day. I'm proud of the fact that all of my friends, except for Sam who married early, went on to college. Most people only remember us for basketball. That's why whenever I'm at any function or event I make this fact known.

After winning our second championship, *The Indianapolis Recorder*, which was the largest Black-owned newspaper in Indiana, feted us with an elaborate celebration. They gave all the players a bronzed shoe. They were given the shoes by our athletic department and they had them bronzed in the form of a trophy. They were really nice, and we were very appreciative. The El Amigo and Cosmo Knight social clubs gave us a banquet. The mayor of Indianapolis issued a proclamation declaring it our day in the city. We were sent telegrams of congratulations from all the city high schools. The ride on a fire truck to Northwestern Park for a bonfire was immediately after we won the game and had left Butler Fieldhouse. Crispus Attucks High School closed for the day, after we had a big rally. People in the neighborhood celebrated also. I can't begin to describe the ongoing show of pride and appreciation they displayed. Our pictures, along with all the championship teams of every state in the country, were in a national magazine. It was truly a memorable time.

Coach Crowe

I remember when we would always go to coach's house during the tournament between games. We would be lying on the couches or the floor on pallets and in chairs. There weren't any hotels in town that we could stay at. Mrs. Betty Crowe would always fix snacks, ice tea, etc. She was always behind him one hundred percent in whatever he had to do for the sake of the team. She was our "first lady." She remains a friend to this day and is always invited and welcomed to any event that is given to honor the team. She used to call us to confirm that we were at home where we were supposed to be (curfew). She had kids of her own, so it had to be a burden on her as far as having time to do it.

He was a fair man but he was hard, and I think that is what made us successful. He was caring as far as what we needed, and he was a disciplinarian. He was reared in Whitestown, Indiana, on a farm with his seven brothers, one who when on to be named Mr. Basketball in Indiana and a professional baseball player with the Cincinnati Reds.

Coach Crowe was raised in a white environment and had little interaction with any Black people. He played basketball with Indiana Central College and met and played against a lot of the people he ended up coaching against. After one year of being an assistant coach, he went on to be the top coach in Indiana high school basketball history as far as winning percentage is concerned, while compiling a record of 179–20. He went on to serve as athletic director at Crispus Attucks High School and then as an Indiana state representative. He also had a brief tenure as head of the Indianapolis Parks Department.

He has two daughters and two sons. One son, Larry, is a sheriff's deputy; the other, Lloyd, is on the police department. His eldest daughter, Katherine, is a retired educator; the youngest, Linda, was married to former NBA star, Billy Knight.

Coach Crowe was never selected Coach of the Year despite his success. He won ninety percent of all the games he coached. Oscar was aware of this and through his insight, he got as many of us together that were available at the time and we presented him with a five-foot trophy proclaiming him as our Coach of the Year and of All Time. He was moved and elated at the gesture. A few of us used to check on him from time to time, and a few still did up until his untimely death in December 2003.

1956 Crispus Attucks State Champions

First Undefeated Team in Indiana Tournament History; W—31, L—0

Front row: Ed Searcy, John Gipson, Odell Donel, Bill Brown, Stanford Patton, Oscar Robertson

Back row: James Enoch, Sam Milton, Levern Benson, Coach Ray Crowe, Herbert Swanigan, Henry Robertson, Al Maxey

Forty-fifth Class Reunion—June 9

During the year of 2001, the Class of 1956 celebrated their forty-fifth reunion, which was held at Riverwalk Banquet Center. Approximately seventy-five of our class members were in attendance, along with another one hundred twenty-five people consisting of other Crispus Attucks classes and friends.

The committee members of the Class of 1955, Tyree Terrell and Pheola (Marion) Akers, also participated and brought along several friends. It was a huge success and brought together classmates who hadn't seen each other in years. Our Mistress of Ceremonies was Suzanne Stantley, a 1967 graduate of Crispus Attucks and also the sister of Maxine (Stantley) Coleman, who was the Class of 1956 reunion committee president.

She did a tremendous job and introduced our special guests, all former Crispus Attucks teachers. Those teachers were Albert Spurlock, Mrs. Doris Bradford, and Mrs. Frances Stout, who all received plaques, in thanks of their contribution to our success in life. Mrs. Paula Coleman, an outstanding opera contralto, performed her superlative rendition of the Lord's Prayer. Her mother-in-law, Maxine Coleman, and all who were present were appreciative and deeply moved by her performance. All of the members of the 1956 championship team, who were present, were honored for their history-making accomplishments in 1956. The five members present who also played on the first championship team in 1955 were Stan Patton, James Enoch, Sam Milton, Bill Brown, and John Gipson. It was truly a memorable evening.

Memories

I think enduring hard times help to build character in a person. It did me. I think going through hard times, doing without things, etc., made me stronger and pushed me to accept a work ethic early in life. When looking back over my life, I can see how working prepared me for just about all of life's trials and constant change. A lot of people I knew gave up easily in just about everything life threw at them. Every time I got knocked down, so to speak, I always got right up and got back into the thick of things. I guess it's not how many times you get set back, it's getting up every time you do. This is very important in competitive sports because only the strong prevail in athletic competition. If you're strong and have heart, you'll prevail or do well. This especially applied to all the Crispus Attucks ball players because of all the obstacles and odds they had to overcome. It's why the all did well in life after the glory days were over.

Stan Patton concurred and also added it gave him the necessary attributes he needed while traveling all over the world and intermingling with different cultures of people. He was always able to blend in wherever he went, just as he did back in the fifties in Indianapolis and Nashville, Tennessee, and Chicago and Los Angeles, California, during the sixties and seventies. He was indeed a people person. As was stated previously, he promotes Crispus Attucks High School in Miami, Florida, where he resides to this day. His displays of pictures, news articles, and artifacts are popular in Miami.

Al Spurlock

Al Spurlock was Coach Crowe's assistant from day one back in 1951. He was the head track coach at Attucks beginning in 1950, and he held the position all the while he assisted Coach Crowe in basketball. He was a graduate of the University of Illinois and the first Black to participate in track in the Big Ten Conference. He was also a big reason for the success of the Attucks basketball program. He would get the basketball players to participate in track and cross country, thus putting them in a position to maintain conditioning all year long. As a result, the basketball team's conditioning never lacked. They were always able to maintain Crowe's fast break style of play, nonstop. This is something the first good team (1951) didn't have, and it showed in the state finals that year.

Al Spurlock was a great teacher, coach, confidante, and a good friend. All the former Attucks players he coached on his reserve teams, a couple of which won the city championship, appreciated him. Some of the players on the championship teams (1955–1956) were standouts on the track team. Oscar and Albert Maxey were good hurdlers. Oscar was high jump champ in the city his senior year. Albert was a standout cross-country runner. Willie Merriweather, Levern Benson, Bill Scott, and Henry Robertson all were members of the track or cross-country teams and did well. Mr. Spurlock was a key to Attucks's success in all its endeavors on the athletic front. We all salute Coach Al Spurlock.

Chapter 13: Championship Celebration

We used to go to dances at the Northwestern Center, which is now known as Watkins Community Center. We were like celebrities and the envy of all the guys when it came to the girls. Once we were supposed to be in our homes on curfew because we had an upcoming game. We went to the center anyway and the coach came in unannounced and busted us. We were disciplined by running laps after practice. We never did that again!

The center was adjacent to Northwestern Park, where we went to a bonfire the night we won our championship to celebrate afterwards. There must have been a few thousand people out there that night. We also were let in to any movie theatre free at any time we chose to go. People were really nice to us, and those are times I'll never forget. Enoch reminded us of the time we were given dozens of donuts to eat by several bakeries. We had so much we had to give them away to kids in the neighborhood.

All the social clubs and several other civic groups gave banquets honoring our accomplishments. I don't think any team today will ever experience what we did back during those times.

During our years at Attucks, we had the entire Black community behind us. Stan Patton made me realize it wasn't just in our individual neighborhoods, but everywhere. The Indiana Avenue area was steadfast in their backing of us. We met lots of individuals who personally went to every home and road game that we played. Julius Griffin was a big fan of Stan Patton. He loved the way he used to fake a man, sometimes almost to the point of falling down.

There were others like George Thomas, who was a successful businessman. He was tops in the insurance industry all over the state of Indiana. Razz Nelson and George Blakely were Avenue king pins who were our staunch supporters. Daniel "Poot Eye" Mason was another supporter, along with the late Forrest Jones, who was a personal friend of mine. He created a barbeque chain of stores in the city and employed lots of people. His son, Ronald, still runs the business today. You could count on these guys along with numerous others, too numerous to name.

Butler Fieldhouse used to be filled to capacity (10,000–15,000) every game we played there. Our other games were played at Tech High School, which held about 3,000 people. All Blacks on every side of town would go to or listen to our games on the radio. They would go about their business at work or whatever bursting with pride over our success on the basketball court. It was just about all they had to look forward to back in those days. Black kids at other high schools used to come to our games and root for us. This is the kind of pride everyone displayed at our accomplishments.

After we won our sectional and regional during tournament time, all the other schools would send one cheerleader from each of their schools to show their support for us when we played in the state finals. This is the only time I have ever heard of this happening down through the years. I guess they wanted to be a part of the first city (Indianapolis) state championship.

Every year at tournament time, Attucks's name pops up whenever a record is equaled or broken that was set back then. They have the class system now that allows for four championships in four categories (1A, 2A, 3A, and 4A). To me, the old system produced a true state champion because you had to go through everybody in the state, not just certain schools. But I guess everything changes, not always for the better.

Stan Patton put it into perspective when he said, "What we did was a 'people' thing. It was by, for, and about the people. It gave our race something to be proud about back then when there was not much else to be proud of during those times."

Ronald Crowe, the brother of Norman Crowe who played at Attucks in 1954, said, "There's nothing like Attucks basketball anywhere. I met guys in the Army who would always question me about it.

Chapter 14: College

I had offers from two Black colleges, Clark in Atlanta and Jackson State in Mississippi. The University of Utah showed interest in me also, but after reviewing all my options, I went out to Indiana Central College as a walk on. They paid my tuition, but I had to live at home. I did well out there, making the varsity my freshman year. Although I was better, I had to give way to a senior just back from the Army and take a bench role. I did well, averaging twelve points a game and dominating the backboards.

I got ineligible and, although I didn't flunk out of school, I was cleared out through admissions by Coach Angus Nicoson so I would always be straight in case I wanted to try school again. In 1985, I went to Martin University to complete my degree and got within one semester of graduating. Working and trying to go to school at a much older age, 48, didn't quite agree with me. I still have my final transcript showing me with a 3.0 out of a 4.0 grade point average (B average).

After I dropped out of school out at Indiana Central, Brown and Patton came home due to medical problems. We sort of just hung out. We would go up to Cincinnati to Oscar's games sometimes. Although we always went up there unannounced, he would always get us seats about five rows behind the Cincinnati bench. His coach would bring the tickets to the door where we would be waiting. Afterwards, he would go with us to Frisch's Big Boy restaurant to eat. Boy, we would really put away some food. That's one thing I could say about Oscar. He never changed because of his star status.

I remember one time he played in an exhibition game against the Detroit Pistons out at the fairgrounds in Indianapolis. The team was headed to the playing floor by way of the hallway where spectators were buying food and congregating. He stopped and greeted my wife and me. Although the team was already on the floor, he spent five minutes or so with us and we really drew a crowd. Some of the people knew I had played with him and understood the relationship we had. He remains a good friend to this day. When I still worked at the Canterbury Hotel, he would stop by every time he was in town and we would catch up on things. People would interrupt us asking for autographs or request having pictures taken with him. He always responded in a gracious, friendly manner. One time we all had dinner with him, but Sam Milton couldn't go because his wife, Carol, was recovering from a serious illness. We all missed Sam's presence. Brown, Patton, and myself enjoyed the evening with Oscar.

John Gipson

We strolled down the downtown streets, and people stopped Oscar for autographs, which he obliged. Kids were yelling out, "Hi Oscar!" We went to a bar and a bunch of guys engaged us in a conversation about basketball. We finished the evening having dinner at a restaurant and then bid Oscar goodbye. He took off for home in Cincinnati.

Chapter 15: Chicago Connection

Stan Patton and I initiated the relationship with the ball players from Chicago. He had met Joe Buckhalter at Tennessee State College in 1956–57, where they were teammates on that first small college National Championship team. Joe invited Stan to Chicago during the summer of 1957 and I went along.

Joe's parents were very hospitable and gracious during our stay there. I'll always be thankful and indebted for their hospitality. We got up every day and went all over Chicago playing basketball. We met all of the great players of the era and enjoyed playing against and with them. I had never seen so many players who could dunk the ball during a game situation. Joe could seemingly go to the top of the backboard from a standing still position. They were more aggressive as players, but we were better shooters and fundamentally sounder. They were constantly trying to block shots and Stan frustrated them with his trickery.

We invited them to Indianapolis to play in the Lockefield Tournament. Stan and I played with them that first year. They came back the next year and won the tournament. They brought along all the top players in Chicago at the time. A few of them were Joe Buckhalter, Willie Jones, Tony Banks, Shellie and Ernie McMillan, McKinley Cowsen, and Floyd "Soup" Campbell.

Ironically, we encountered a couple of them at an event the NCAA Hall of Champions put on featuring our championship teams and their Great Dusable team out of Chicago. It was good to see them again. I got to see Fabulous "Sweet" Charlie Brown again. We joked about having met in The Presidents nightclub back in 1957 when Patton and I first went to Chicago.

Most of his teammates are now deceased. Their coach was able to be present, although he and our coach were both in wheelchairs. He was a nice guy and seemed to still harbor feelings of resentment about the racial overtones that deprived his team of winning a championship back then. Charlie Brown said he was going to work toward putting on the same type of event involving both of our ball clubs in the near future. All of my teammates who were present signed a thank you card, and we sent one to both George Smith and Bill Rhoden. We all thought we were fortunate to be around to participate in such a historical event. Our heartfelt thanks and appreciation go out to both George Smith for hosting the event and Bill Rhoden for coming all the way from New York to cover it.

Chapter 16:
Ray Crowe All-Stars

After our high school and college careers had finished, we got together a team and called it the Ray Crowe All-Stars. We played in several outdoor tournaments during the summer and dominated them. We won at Logansport, Elwood, Lockefield (Indianapolis), and several other small towns. Our team consisted of Bill Brown, Willie Merriweather, Winford O'Neal, Bill Mason, Bill Hampton, Bill Scott, Norman Crowe, Bob Jewell, Don Thomas, and myself. I don't think we lost a game that year. All the top players in the state used to get teams together to try to beat us. Willie Gardner was our coach.

A couple of our friends who played at Shortridge High School played with us during the tournament at Elwood, Indiana. It was the first time we had ever played organized ball on the same team with them. They were Herschell Turner and Bobby Williams. Bobby was a little All-American at St. Joseph College in Rensselaer, Indiana. Herschell was an All-Big Eight player at the University of Nebraska and played in the American Basketball League for two years. When the league folded, he joined the Harlem Globetrotters. It was a good year (1959).

During the summer of 1959, Bill Brown, Stan Patton, "Easy" Ed Hurt, Ronald Crowe, and several other guys went to Evanston, Illinois, to play in an outdoor tournament. Sonny Boyd, who was with the YMCA, took the team up there. I had dental work done the day they left and didn't get to go. They did pretty good playing against some of Chicago's top players. Willie "The Bird" Jones, Art Hicks, Tony Banks, Mac Cowsen, "Soup" Campbell, and a host of others represented Chicago. Stan Patton had an outstanding game for his team. They lost by two points. But they really gained the respect of the Chicago players that day. It is ironic how our paths crossed with the guys from

Chicago over the years, after Patton and I had initially met them. When the guys came back, they told me they thought they could have won the game if I had been there. That really showed me what type of game I had, after that comment.

Chicago was a mecca and still is when it comes to putting out outstanding players that go on to another level in the sport. Joe Buckhalter told me the first Chicago players to play in the NBA were "Nat" Sweetwater Clifton of the Globetrotters, Johnny "Red" Kerr, Willie "The Bird" Jones, Shellie McMillan, and Joe himself, who played for the Globetrotters and the Cincinnati Royals. The Minneapolis Lakers drafted "Sweet" Charlie Brown of Chicago Dusable High School and Seattle University.

All of those younger Chicago players were big fans of Willie Gardner, who joined the Globetrotters in Chicago in 1954. He was a legend there and dominated with the Globetrotters. Most recently, in March of 2003, Meadowlark Lemon retired as a Globetrotter, mentioning Willie while appearing on *The Best Damned Sports Show Period.* He said Willie was the best player they had at the time and could dunk three basketballs at the same time.

Chapter 17:
Goose Tatum

A friend of mine, Cleveland Harp, who played at Attucks three years before I did, came by my house one day in 1961. He recruited me to play on a team with him called "Goose" Tatum's All-Star Team. I went to Chicago to try out and made the team. We had some pretty good players from all across the country. Some of the notables were Ellis Appling from Detroit, who played collegiate ball at the University of Pan American at Texas; Art Hicks; Hank Gunter of Seton Hall; my high school teammate, Bill Brown; and several others from New York, Ohio, and Oklahoma. It was a good experience, and it also confirmed my belief that I could play with the best players in the country. Satchel Paige, the baseball great and legend, coached the team that traveled and played against Goose's team. He was something special, always coming up with little sayings and quotes. He was a walking history buff.

Goose thought a lot of my game and told me I was a pretty good shooter. I can see why he and the other original Globetrotters used to beat NBA teams on a regular basis. He was a fantastic pivot player as he had a good hook shot and was a superb passer. My friend Stan Patton got some of his passes and moves from Goose. Goose isn't given the credit, but he is one of the all-time best players to ever play the game of basketball.

I remember once at one of our tryout camps in Chicago, some of the Harlem Globetrotters came by. They had heard Goose was having a camp and stopped by to say hello to him. During the course of the conversation, Goose asked them to scrimmage against us so he could get a better idea of what kind of players he had. We ran them into the ground. One of them told Goose they had been out late and didn't have much sleep and that's why they hadn't fared so well against us. It was an experience, and I was mildly surprised at how easily we had handled them. I guess if you've got game, you can play with anybody.

Touring with Goose Tatum

Once when I was touring with Goose Tatum, we were traveling by chartered bus and Goose was traveling in his Cadillac Eldorado, driven by one of the players, Spike. The bus carrying the players got separated from Goose in a snowstorm. Goose never made it to the scheduled game, which was in northern Ohio. He called ahead to the hotel we were booked in and left word for Satchel Paige to call him when we made it in. He instructed Satchel to go ahead with the game without him.

Tiny Brown, who went under the name Goose Tatum Jr., was instructed to do the Goose show during the game. He asked to speak to me and told me to go to the cashier's office, introduce myself, and then after the game pick up the gate receipts. I was told not to count it or open the bags, but to give it to him at our next stop. I was surprised he picked me out of the group to take care of his business. He was being audited by the IRS at each game for back taxes owed the government. He could only receive whatever was left after the government agent counted the receipts and took their share. He called ahead, and they were expecting me after the game to pick up Goose's share. Everything went off as planned, and at the next stop, I gave him that day's receipts. By Satchel's reaction, I got the feeling he resented the fact Goose picked me to take care of this business instead of him. He made snide remarks when Goose wasn't around, saying Goose didn't care about anybody regardless of what was done for him. After he saw that it didn't mean anything to me and that I wasn't trying to win his favor, he got over it. We still had a pretty good relationship thereafter. A lot of the guys had little remarks they made about the situation, but I didn't let it bother me and they got over it, too, after they saw I didn't try to gain Goose's favor in anyway. I felt good that Goose would even think that much of me to let me handle such a large sum of cash money for him like that.

I had previously driven him and his family to one of the games in his car, following the bus. He got to question me about things, and when I told him I had played with Oscar in high school and also played in college, he was surprised and impressed. We only had six guys that had college experience, and the rest were people he picked up at community centers and places like that. He was impressed that I had a regular job at home, and had done some of the things I had done. He told me, "You're different from the rest of these guys." He compensated me for taking care of that little business for him, and I never told anybody what he gave me. I overheard him telling Satchel Paige about me, saying, "That old tall boy can really shoot it." He was surprised when I told him I was quitting when we arrived in Detroit, Michigan. I told him my sister had told me by phone that my employer at Hygrade Meat Packing Company had recalled me back to work by telegram. He wished me well, and I went back home to work. I got to see him two years later when they played a game here in town out at Indiana Central College, where I had played. That was the last time I ever saw him. He would eventually pass in the year 1968. It was a big loss to the sports world.

After doing extensive research and reading, I found out that Goose was really a good basketball player. He played outstanding against the college All-Americans during the Globetrotters tour against them. He also did well against the top professional players of those times, before the Globetrotters started doing their "show" during the games. I was told that only after Willie Gardner arrived to play with the Globetrotters did his playing time in the pivot position decline. It was an honor for me to know him and play for him.

Chapter 18: Helping Bring About Social Change

After winning our second state championship, you could see things starting to change a little. Where Blacks used to have to sit in the balcony of a movie theatre, they could now sit anywhere. Many a time Brown, Enoch, Sam, and I would go to a show and never have to pay. They saw we were gentlemen and always carried ourselves so whenever we were in public. They were glad to be able to tell people they saw us and actually talked to us. We were like celebrities.

Blacks used to have to get anything they ordered in a restaurant to-go. They couldn't sit down and eat it. There weren't many Black restaurants to go to. We were the first Blacks to sit down in a restaurant downtown and eat. We went to Fendrick's Restaurant for a victory dinner following our winning the first state championship in 1955. A lot of places that Blacks weren't allowed in, we went to, but only because of the fact they knew who we were.

That wasn't right, but it was a start. Whenever we would be standing on a corner thumbing a ride, whites started picking us up and giving us a ride, sometimes all the way to our destination. They were glad to be in our company. I remember the times before this, they wouldn't even look our way, and if they did, they would hurriedly lock their car doors. Things have gone back to this way, only because of concern for one's personal safety. Also, the renting of prime banquet and meeting places to Blacks became more available.

Chapter 19: Crispus Attucks Impact on Basketball in the Fifties

Back in 1951, a big scandal evolved in college and professional basketball. Some of the top players in the country, through professional gamblers, were shaving points in games to dictate and control the point spread. This brought the integrity of the game to a new low. Attendance slacked off and people became less interested in the sport.

About three years after the scandal, a college team from out west, the University of San Francisco Dons, won two straight national titles while going undefeated. The team featured two outstanding players, Bill Russell and K.C. Jones. This all happened in 1955 and 1956, the same years Crispus Attucks accomplished their feats. This had never been done before, especially involving Black players and an all-Black team.

Blacks at that time were said to be incapable of performing under pressure in an official situation. These feats put all these myths to rest. What firmly validated the fact that they could do these things was the three-year national championship run (1957, 1958, and 1959) put together by Tennessee State University.

This team featured Dick Barnett, the Indiana All-Star player who played for Gary Roosevelt High School in 1955 against Crispus Attucks in the state championship game. After leading Tennessee State to three titles and being named MVP three times, he went on to star for the Cleveland Pipers professional basketball team under his college coach, Johnny McLendon, who was the first Black professional basketball coach. He went on to play for the Syracuse Nationals in the NBA and finished his career with the New York Knicks, winning the NBA Championship.

Johnny McLendon was instrumental in the development and promotion of basketball in the United States. His fast break style of play was the same used at Crispus Attucks and Gary Roosevelt high schools.

The great Chicago Dusable team that was robbed of its place in history used this same tempo style of play, although they were more flashy.

It is ironic that these three small teams all enjoyed success during the same period of time. This made the major colleges start looking at and seeking Black players to join their respective programs. They realized that if they wanted to win, they had to use them. This was definitely so on the professional level.

I must add that, in 1956, Evansville Lincoln High School in Indiana went undefeated during the regular season but lost in the tournament. A Black man, Art Taylor, coached them. Two of their players went on to play for Tennessee State College during its championship years. One was a guy named Merriweather and the other was John Barnhill, who played on the championship teams.

Chapter 20: Crispus Attucks Accomplishments

Years 1951–1957

- Won six sectional crowns in seven years
- Won six regional crowns in seven years
- Won four semi-state crowns in seven years
- Runners up one time (final game) (1957)
- Lost in morning game of finals (1951)
- Won Indianapolis's first state championship (1955)
- First all-Black team to win a state crown in the country (1955)
- First Indiana team to be ranked nationally (1955)
- First undefeated team to win the state crown
- Voted the second-best team in the country in the fifties and sixties (1956 team)
- Only high school team known to win a championship without having a gym

In the year 2000, sports writers selected the 1955 state championship basketball team as one of the Top Ten Sports Stories of the Twentieth Century. Crispus Attucks was ranked number seven. Attucks, along with the Milan 1954 "miracle" team, were the only high schools selected.

Coach Ray Crowe had a record of 179 wins and 20 losses in seven years. That's the best winning percentage in history. Attucks had eight players named to the Indiana All-Star Team during Crowe's seven years. Two were named Mr. Basketball.

- 1951–Robert Jewell
- 1953–Bailey Robertson, alternate
- 1953–Hallie Bryant, Mr. Basketball

- 1954–Bill Mason
- 1955–Willie Merriweather
- 1956–Oscar Robertson, Mr. Basketball
- 1956–Stan Patton, alternate
- 1957–Al Maxey
- 1958–Edgar Searcy

Oscar Robertson—Crispus Attucks Legend

- Two-time state champ (1955, 1956)
- Mr. Basketball of Indiana (1956)
- All-Star Team (1956)
- High School All-American (1955, 1956)
- College All-American (1958, 1959, 1960)
- Led nation in scoring three years (1958, 1959, 1960)
- College Player of the Year (1958, 1959, 1960)
- Pan American gold medalist (1959)
- Olympic gold medalist (1960)
- NBA Rookie of the Year (1961)
- NBA MVP (1964)
- MVP of All-Star Game (3 times)
- All-Pro NBA player (12 years)
- Averaged a triple double in NBA (3 years)
- Voted to Indiana Highs School Basketball Hall of Fame (1981)
- Named to Silver Anniversary Team (1981)
- First basketball player to appear on the cover of Time magazine
- Selected to Naismith Basketball Hall of Fame (1979)
- Named one of the NBA's Greatest of All-Time

- Union president for the League Players Association (11 years)
- Successfully led a judicial challenge that created player free agency (known as the Robertson Rule)

Other Crispus Attucks Legends

Bailey Robertson

Played on the Indiana All-Star Team in 1953. He played four years at Attucks and hit the shot (as a sophomore) that launched the Attucks dynasty. He played four years at the former Indiana Central College and set the following records:

- Most career points (2,280)
- Scored thirty or more points (19 times)
- Most points scored in a season (754)
- Best career scoring average (23.2 ppg)
- Best season scoring average (28.7 ppg)
- Team MVP for three straight years
- Hoosier College All-Conference for three straight years

Bailey Robertson

He played for the Globetrotters for two years and was inducted into the Indiana Basketball Hall of fame in 1990.

"Wee" Willie Gardner

Ranked as one of the top big men in Indiana basketball history. As a sophomore, he led Crispus Attucks High School to the state finals in 1951. Academic eligibility led to his only playing two years in high school. He was named

All-State two years. He was elected to the Indiana Hall of Fame in 1977.

He played with the Harlem Globetrotters, helping them capture the World Series of Basketball title against the College All-Americans in 1954 and 1957. He was named the game's Most Valuable Player both times. He signed with the New York Knicks in April of 1957. He never played for the Knicks during the regular season (exhibition only) as a heart impairment required him to retire for health reasons.

The Indiana Hall of Fame named him to the Silver Anniversary Team in 1977. He received his Legends Globetrotter ring during a special halftime ceremony at Market Square Arena in Indianapolis on January 17, 1998.

Hallie Bryant

Hallie Bryant

Played three years of varsity at Attucks. Led the city in scoring three years, was named Mr. Basketball in 1953, and played on the Indiana All-Star Team in 1953. He played at Indiana University and earned All-Big Ten Honors in 1957. He played for the Globetrotters for thirteen years and was advanced to public relations manager for the Globetrotters thereafter, which he did for fourteen years.

Bill Mason

Played two years of varsity at Attucks, 1953 and 1954. He carried his team to the semi-state tournament in 1954 and was named an All-State selection in 1954. He was selected to the Indiana All-Star Team in 1954 and played with the Ray Crowe All-Stars for two years.

Robert Jewell

Played on the state finalist team in 1951. He won the coveted Trester Award in 1951, was named All-State in

1951, and played on the Indiana All-Star Team in 1951. He played at University of Michigan in 1953 and played three years at Indiana Central College in 1954, 1955, and 1956. He was named All-Conference two years, 1954 and 1956. He is deceased.

Willie Merriweather

Crispus Attucks Indiana State Champion in 1955. He was named an Indiana All-Star in 1955 (high school) and a Purdue University All-American in 1959. He played in the continental league for twelve years (semipro). He was named to the Indiana Basketball Hall of Fame. He is now the retired principal of a Detroit, Michigan, high school and a retired NBA players agent.

Bill Brown

Crispus Attucks two-time state champ in 1955 and 1956. He was an Indiana All-State selection in 1955 and 1956. He holds the Indiana State Tourney rebound record (1956) and played on Tennessee State University's National Championship team. He played in the Eastern League for five years (semipro) with the Astronauts.

John Gipson

Two-time state champion in 1955 and 1956. He played at Indiana Central College in 1957 and 1958. He played on a city AAU championship team and played with Goose Tatum's All-Star Team. He retired from the Daimler Chrysler Corporation. He then worked at the Canterbury Hotel, where he received the Rose Award, the highest award given in the hospitality industry in the state of Indiana. He retired from the Canterbury in 2013.

Bill Scott

Indiana State Champion in 1955 and an All-State selection in 1955. He attended Franklin College and was named All-Conference in 1956. He then attended Butler University and was co-captain and MVP in 1958 and 1959. He was named All-Conference and was Butler's first MVP and Hilton U. Brown winner simultaneously. During his time at Butler, he was the team's leading scorer with twenty points per game. He coached and taught school in the public school system for forty years. He was inducted into the Indiana Basketball Hall of Fame in 2012. He passed away in 1996.

Bill Hampton

Indiana State Champion in 1955 and an All-State selection in 1955. He attended Indiana Central College and was All-Conference for two years. He is a retired insurance agency owner, retired deputy sheriff, and retired owner of Hampton & Hampton Building Maintenance. He was inducted into the Indiana Basketball Hall of Fame in 2017.

Stanford Patton

Two-time state champion in 1955 and 1956. He was an All-State selection in 1956 and an Indiana All-Star in 1956. He played on the Tennessee State University National Champion teams in 1957 and 1958. He is a retired political activist and history curator of CAHS athletics.

Sheddrick Mitchell

Two-time state champion in 1955. He was an All-State selection in 1955. He played at Butler University for two years and was an All-Navy selection while in special services. He received his BS and BA degrees in economics from Bryant College in Springfield, Rhode Island. He was also a HUD fellow at American University. In 2015, he joined other members of the Crispus Attucks championship team as Grand Marshals of the Indianapolis 500 Festival Parade. He passed away in 2019.

Samuel Milton

Two-time state champion in 1955 and 1956. He retired from General Motors Corporation. He received the Rose Award while working for the Ritz Charles Restaurant for being an outstanding host to its patrons. He is deceased.

James Enoch

Played on the 1956 state championship team. He played at Clark College in Atlanta, Georgia. He retired from McDonnell Douglas Aircraft Corporation. He also played with the Cleveland Harps semipro team.

Edgar Searcy

Played on the state championship team in 1956, the state runner up team in 1957, and the state finalist team in 1958. He was an All-State selection in 1957 and 1958 and an Indiana All-Star in 1958. He played at the University of Illinois for two years and finished at the University of Southern Illinois. He retired from Eli Lilly as an executive and was an attorney in Indianapolis. He is deceased.

Henry Robertson

Played on the state championship team in 1956. He went to the University of Cincinnati. He retired from the State Parole Board in Cincinnati.

John Clemons

Played on the state championship team in 1956. He retired from Link Belt Corporation.

Herbert Swanigan

Played on the state championship team in 1956. He retired from International Harvester. He is deceased.

Levern Benson

Played on the state championship team in 1956, the state runner up team in 1957, and the state finalist team in 1958. He played on the Ohio All-Star Team in 1958. He played at Miami of Ohio University for three years, where he was an honorable mention All-American and an All-Conference selection his senior year. He played on the National Industrial League Championship team. He was inducted into the Indiana Basketball Hall of Fame in 2014. He is now retired in Denver, Colorado.

Albert Maxey

Played on the state championship team in 1956 and the state runner up team in 1957. He played at the University of Nebraska from 1958 through 1961 and was named All-Conference two years. He is currently a detective on the Lincoln, Nebraska, police force.

Odell Donel

Played on the state championship team in 1956 and the state runner up team in 1957. He is deceased.

Johnny Mack Brown

Played on the state championship team in 1955. Was an All-City football selection. He is deceased.

Willie Burnley

Played on the state championship team in 1955 and the semi-state team in 1954. He played at Wilberforce College in 1956. He is deceased.

Chapter 21: Lockefield Dustbowl Tournament

Prior to making the varsity at Attucks, we all used to go to the Lockefield Tournament to see the games. We stayed all day for two days, Friday and Saturday. The place would be packed solid, and it looked as if every sports fan in the city was there. There were refreshment stands and people selling pop, beer, and so on from their cars.

Some of the top players of the time would come to compete there. Entee Shine and Joe Bertrand from Notre Dame, Don Schlundt from Indiana University, and Sam Richardson and John Bridgeforth from Indiana State College competed on their teams. A one-armed guy from Gary, Indiana, and a member of the Harlem Globetrotters were crowd favorites whenever they played. The guy from Gary could rebound with his one arm.

A few white teams would come in to play; although they usually had one or two good players, they were never able to win the tournament. There were guys off the street who never played organized or school ball who could and would, most of the time, eliminate the white teams from the tournament. John Bridgeforth, a former Attucks player, brought a team consisting of his teammates at ISU, Sam Richardson, and several other top players in the city of Indianapolis. Binkie Brown from Indiana Central defeated the top amateur and collegians from four states to win the tournament in 1954.

We would watch in earnest, learn and dream at playing there in the near future ourselves. It was comparable to Rucker Park in New York City. Although, I think more New York players went on to the next level of playing during the later years when the white colleges started accepting Black players.

We had players with nicknames such as Boo, Chick Entree, Ox, R.J., Eddie Baby, Smooth Dan, and others. It was sort of a proving ground and a measuring stick as to whether you had game or not. If you had one, it would show, but if you didn't have a game, it would also show.

During the summer of 1956, I played in the Lockefield Tourney for the first time. An older guy named Tommy Ryle asked me to play on a team he had gotten together off the playground. They didn't have any size and were just fair players. I was the biggest man on the team at six feet five inches. The opposing team was made up of former high school and college players. There was Bob Jewell of Attucks and Central College, Bailey League of Attucks and North Carolina University, Howard League of Attucks and Texas Southern University, Sam Richardson of South Bend Central High School and Indiana State University, and several other real good players. I was playing the center position on defense and forward on offense. This was because my guys were intimidated and wouldn't take their shots. I started off good and kept us in the game. They maintained good defensive posture, which was another reason we stayed within striking distance. Jewell tried to guard me but couldn't do the job. I hit about five straight jump shots from the corner on him, and Sam Richardson asked to switch on me. It was to no avail, as I drove on him for baskets and sometimes went outside to hit long jump shots. It was the first time I had a chance to show what I was capable of doing. Most people in the crowd were surprised at how I almost pulled the game out for us. We only lost by one point and should have gotten the ball for one last play, but the referee (Ronald Crowe) called it in their favor. I scored thirty-one points during that game and gained respectability that day, citywide. Benny Cook, an Attucks star on the 1951 team, congratulated me and made the statement, "You're finally going to do something." I replied, "You can't do anything sitting on the bench." The whole crowd was seemingly cheering for me that day. I guess it was because we were the underdogs.

Oscar, Maxey, Brown, Henry, and several others had a team that went on to win the tournament. They were simply outstanding, as was to be expected. Hallie Bryant and Bailey Robertson were in the crowd and didn't play because of college rules stating that no college players actively playing in school could play in nonsanctioned tournaments. During the summer of 1953 following their graduation, Hallie, Bailey, and Willie Gardner won the tournament on a team sponsored by Joe Stuart of Stuart Mortuary, Incorporated. They dominated the tourney, defeating teams from the city, state, and midwestern parts of the country.

Prather's Hot Shots, 1963 Lockefield Dustbowl Champions

Back, left to right: Bobby Edmonds, John Gipson, Herschell Turner, Coach Bobby Prather, Dick Cook

Front, left to right: Larry McIntyre, "Easy Ed" Hurt, Chester "Tricky Lew" Lewis, Jerry Trice, Bruiser Gaines

During the summer of 1960, we had a team that won the Lockefield Tournament. We beat teams from Gary, Indiana; Illinois; South Bend, Indiana; Milwaukee, Wisconsin; and teams from all over the state of Indiana. Our good friend, Joe Buckhalter from Chicago, led us and would later go on to play for the Harlem Globetrotters and the Cincinnati Royals of the NBA. He played collegiately at Tennessee A&I College in Nashville, Tennessee.

He dominated the boards and did some unbelievable dunks never seen before during those times. Bill Brown, Stan Patton, Jim Enoch, James Haywood, Fred McCoy, Melvin Woods, Ed Hurt, Herschell Turner, Henry Robertson, and myself made up the team. I also played on a team coached by my good friend, Bobby Prather, who won the tournament in 1963. Bobby is now deceased.

Chapter 22: Life After School

In the fall of 1962, Bill Brown and I went to Terre Haute, Indiana, with "Easy" Ed Hurt to play in a game held at Indiana State College against a semipro team. It just so happened that Oscar and Joe Buckhalter, who were playing with the Cincinnati Royals, played an exhibition game against the Detroit Pistons on the same night there. We were the undercard, playing the game before them.

After winning our game and staying over to see Oscar and Joe play, we traveled on to Chicago with Easy Ed to participate in a tryout with his team. They were called the Harlem Clowns, a team which was assembled by one of the original Harlem Globetrotters. His name was Runt Pullens. He wasn't expecting Brown and I, but he was still nice enough to put us up in a hotel and give us meal money for the two days we were there.

Easy introduced us, and when Runt found out who we were he welcomed us with open arms. Brown and I stood out at the camp. All the guys there, who were from New York, New Jersey, and other cities in the Midwest, took notice of us. I had an exceptional camp and was really hitting my shot. After it was over, Runt called us into his office individually and gave us the rundown on his selections. He told me he already had planned to hire his nephew but was glad I had come to the camp and for me to look forward to hearing from him in the near future. We stayed in Chicago and partied with all the guys until they left to go on tour the following day. We went back home to Indianapolis. Brown hooked up with the semipro team in the Eastern League called the Astronauts. He played with them for a few years before joining the fire department.

During the fall of 1963, I got married to my wife, Rebecca Thomas, and had settled down, working at Hygrade Meat Packing company. The company had dropped its old name, which was Kingan Meat Packing, and renamed it Hygrade. Runt sent me a letter to come join the team (Harlem Clowns). I pondered on it a few days and sent him a reply declining the offer. He had been impressed with my offensive skills against the bigger players from New York, who stood six feet ten inches tall. I never regretted the decision and resigned my play to the AAU League. Easy Ed went on to continue playing for another five years with the Clowns.

During the summer of 1963, I played in the Lockefield Dustbowl Tourney on a team coached by my good friend, Bobby Prather, who is now deceased. Bobby Joe Edmonds and Larry McIntyre, who propelled the 1959 Crispus Attucks team to the state championship, led us. They both played collegiately at Tennessee State University. Larry played some AAU ball for a while, then got married and settled down, working for Allison Diesel Motors. They were

1959 Crispus Attucks state championship team with Coach Bill Garrett (back left), Bobby Joe Edmonds (43), and Larry McIntyre (15).

both coached at Attucks by Bill Garrett, an All-American player with Indiana University who played for the Harlem Globetrotters before going on to coach high school basketball in Indianapolis.

Bobby played on the first Indiana Pacers team in the American Basketball Association (ABA). He did well, and after his playing career ended, he opened a cosmetology business in Indianapolis. He died in 1989.

Herschell Turner of Shortridge High School played with us, along with Bobby Eldred, another Tennessee State Player; Stanley Richardson; Chester Lewis; and Paul Henry, another Shortridge High School player who went on to play for the University of Southern Illinois. We had a good team and dominated the tournament that year.

After this period of time, more playing opportunities became available with the starting up of the ABA. The success of this league would eventually cause a merger with the NBA. The presence of such ABA stars as Julius Irving, Moses Malone, George Gervin, Roger Brown, and Mel Daniels caused this merger because the NBA realized the ABA had the more colorful players and posed a threat to the continued success of the NBA.

In 1964, Bill Hampton came by my house to recruit me for a game with a team he played on called the Westlane Drugs All-Stars. Several top collegians played on the team, such as Jack Noone of Marian College here in the city, and others that I hadn't met. We were to play the team at the Pendleton Reformatory consisting of inmates incarcerated there which featured Goose Ligon, a former high school star in Kokomo, Indiana, and also a former Globetrotter. I was never really comfortable the whole time we were there, but I still had a good game. I guarded Goose, and it was a challenge because I had heard so much about him. Bill Hampton was his usual proficient self as he riddled their defense with his outside jump shots. Goose scored forty-eight points and they won the game by eight points. I couldn't hold him defensively, but I scored thirty-five points against him. I felt pretty good about this because I hadn't played any ball in a while. Also, a lot of guys in the stands that I knew got to see me against one of the best around during those times. It was a good experience, but not one I would care to do again.

Chapter 23: Memories

John Gipson

My uncle told me he was at work the afternoon it was determined we were to play Gary Roosevelt in the championship game of the 1955 state final. He overheard some white men say, "Our niggers will beat their niggers," referring to us beating Gary. He wasn't appalled, but he didn't say anything because he was in a no-win situation. He could have possibly lost his job and gotten locked up for starting an altercation. The incidents just go on and on.

The time that we beat Muncie Central in the supposedly "Dream Game," we were leaving the floor, headed to the locker room, when a white cheerleader from Muncie Central High School said while crying, "That's all right, you niggers. We'll beat you next year."

I guess the success we were having that year just brought out the worst in people (opposing fans). Through it all, we just kept our cool and carried ourselves in a way our people would be proud of us. We were winning, so that kind of balanced things out, keeping things on an even keel. The one thing we did demonstrate when we lost the one game in 1955 was taking the loss while displaying class afterwards. We congratulated the guys from Connersville and moved on. I think they knew what the results would have been on a dry floor. After talking with several of the guys I played with at Attucks, I was surprised to learn that not one player was assisted in pursing or answering any scholarship offers. I guess the teachers responsible (counselors) didn't figure we were college material. I understand that we were responsible for our own being, but I just thought the accomplishments that we achieved would warrant some attention to what our possibilities might be as far as whether we would try to go to school or not. In defense of the teachers, I can say they did their job well teaching in the classroom, while demanding excellence in the process. They couldn't get jobs in any other schools at that time. They were definitely qualified in that they all possessed master's degrees along with their bachelor's degrees. I guess they had to stick to the curriculum the City Education Board gave them and not stray from it because Black history was not a priority subject.

It was offered, but the only things they told us about were Booker T. Washington and George Washington Carver. I myself learned in later years about other significant Blacks, like Paul Robeson, Walter White, the Tuskegee Airmen, Madame C.J. Walker, Ms. Mary McLeod Bethune, and others. Like I previously stated, one had to look out for one's self or be left by the wayside. I was surprised when Oscar and Willie Merriweather were said to have gotten their own scholarships without any help or advice.

I remember, when during our practices at Attucks, I used to end up trying to guard Oscar (1956). No one else wanted to try. I would always watch how he would look at the man's eye that was guarding him. He would look you away from a pass he was going to throw one way by looking the opposite way. He had great peripheral vision and could see all over the floor. If you crossed one leg over the other while in defensive pursuit of him, he would do what they call the cross over today and go the other way, leaving you behind in pursuit of him. He could look at you when he was on defense and know your next move eighty-five percent of the time. There were a lot of little, subtle things he did on the court that nobody else was aware of. These are some of the things that made him what he was in the sport. I guess you could say he made a science of the game. One thing I'll go out on a limb and say about him is that he always looked for the best option, and most of the time that was to look, to pass first, and shoot second. I think that having the opportunity to play with him was the best thing that could have happened to me while I tried to play the game of basketball. I'm just sorry he never got to see me at my best in my years after high school.

During the summer of 1956, Bill Brown and I were asked to do some volunteer work with grade school boys. I forget who asked, maybe the Parks Department or the YMCA. We accepted and worked with about seventy-five boys, instructing them on basketball fundamentals and other aspects of the game. A friend, Ollie Daniels, used to let Brown drop him off at work and use his car during the day. It was a godsend because we didn't have transportation. It was fun working with the kids, and a few of them went on to become good high school basketball players. We didn't realize it at the time, but what we did changed a few of the kids' outlook on life. They stayed on the straight path rather than going to a life of crime and extended stints of incarceration. I can't think of anything better we could have done with our time. Ironically, I ended up doing volunteer work coaching youth.

Albert Maxey

Albert made the varsity during his junior year in 1956 and eventually became a starter on the 1956 undefeated championship team. His aggressiveness on defense was his main contribution to the team. He played the point guard position when we played a zone defense during games. He would follow the ball all around the floor as it was passed from position to position. He never got tired when doing so. He had a stellar season in his senior year in 1957. He led the team all the way to the final game, but they came up short, losing to South Bend Central High School.

He was selected to the 1957 All-Star Team and had two good games against the Kentucky All-Star Team. He went on to attend Nebraska University, where he was an All-Conference Big 8 player. He remained in Lincoln, Nebraska, after college and went on to become a law enforcement officer, attaining the rank of captain. He was later selected to the Indiana Basketball Hall of Fame. His wife, who is deceased, was a top educator in the Lincoln school system.

Shortly after she passed, the Lincoln School Board named a school after her, the Joann Maxey Elementary School. He has a daughter who is currently the women's head track coach at Illinois State University. Albert is also a devout alumnus of Crispus Attucks High School and participates in any function that has to do with the celebration of its athletic successes.

Oscar Robertson

He was instrumental in making free agency possible in the NBA. Before playing in the NBA, he had a clause inserted in his contract with the Cincinnati Royals that gave him the right to approve or disapprove where he was to be traded, if and when a trade should come about. This insight enabled him to eventually wind up in Milwaukee, playing alongside Lew Alcindor Abdul-Jabbar, where they ended up winning an NBA Championship in 1971. He also went to court challenging the NBA on the free agency issue and won the lawsuit that granted players the right to go to any team that would sign them if they couldn't reach an agreement with their team. This is called the "Oscar Robertson Law." The players that came after him in the league owe him, to some degree, because he made it possible for them to have negotiating rights, which older players never had. As I stated previously, he always stands firm for what he believes in and will fight to the end for it.

Of all the players ever to play in the NBA, I think most of them will concur that he has done the most to make it possible for players to share in decision making and financial gains. During a short tenure as a TV analyst, he was criticized along with Bill Russell for making comments concerning the referees making bad calls during games. He just told it like it was, and you can see the difference in officiating then and now.

When asked about the comparison of Indiana players versus New York or East Coast players, he said the only difference was they show boat and lean toward being flashy on the court. He told of an experience with two players of the old ABA and one with the NBA who invited him to play some pick-up ball with them in Ohio. He said he gave them a rude awakening and schooled them to the point that they lost some of their cockiness. I always did say if you're a ball player, the real deal is you can play with anyone. Oscar is loyal to Crispus Attucks High School. Whenever he is asked to be a part of something or contribute his time to charities, events, etc., he always is willing if the asker is willing to contribute to the Crispus Attucks Museum. A lot of other athletes don't display this kind of loyalty and are of the kind who forget where they came from.

He was so well-liked as a person that some of us would go by and check on his father, talking to him and spending time with him. A friend named Buddy Rogan was the one who was dedicated to this gesture. I'd worked with Mr. Robertson at the defunct Hygrade Meat Packing plant. He showed me the ropes there and that's how I got to be close with him, especially after he found out I went to college with his oldest son Bailey out at Indiana Central College in 1957. I went by to see him when I wasn't working, and if I couldn't make it, I knew Buddy Rogan would be there. Oscar was very appreciative of our concern for his father.

Oscar Robertson with John Gipson's son, Julian.

Stan Patton

No one in my family ever graduated from high school. They were sharecroppers down in Tennessee. My father couldn't make it here and he went back to the farm in Tennessee.

My mother's sole purpose for her children was to graduate. So she didn't go back. She did her best to raise five boys and one girl. She would clean white people's houses as her livelihood. She was a good worker and earned the respect of all of her employers. We didn't have a lot and often had to survive on sandwiches, cereal, etc., and often had to do without.

Once a friend of mine named Ollie Daniels came to my house, and after seeing our living conditions said to me, "Boy, they need to send you a care package." We didn't have any running water in the house and were often without lights. Through his teasing about my shortcomings, I gained strength to persevere through all the deplorable conditions I had to live with.

I was selected to go to Washington, D.C., as a representative of my grade school (No. 87) during my eighth grade year. After experiencing that trip, I was motivated to strive to be the best I could be. That's why I am so proud, appreciative, and thankful for all I have, and what I've become as a man today.

Another teammate who played on the team was Herbert "Buzzy" Swanigan. He came to Attucks from School No. 37, which was a middle school that went to grade nine. He was an outstanding player there and was something of a legend at the school. We became good friends, and though he never expressed the feeling, he was disappointed in never getting much playing time while he was on the Crispus Attucks varsity team. Coach Crowe did see to it that he got his championship ring. That had to mean something to him. Also, the fact that he was a part of something that was a first in Indiana basketball should have made his experience bittersweet. He graduated in January during the middle of the school year. He got a job at International Harvester, where he worked for thirty years. He has since retired and is enjoying his retirement with his wife, who was also his high school sweetheart.

Chapter 24: The Later Years

Much is said about how athletes on the high school and college level mostly go on to be underachievers in life or failures. I did research on all of the Attucks athletes that played under Coach Crowe and came up with the following information on what they did after their playing days. The list is incomplete, and my apologies go out to **all** who were omitted, mainly because I could not find any information on their whereabouts.

- **Oscar Robertson** attended the University of Cincinnati. He played in the NBA and became a businessman, spokesman, and speaker.
- **Edgar Searcy** attended the University of Southern Illinois. He became a certified public accountant and attorney.
- **Al Maxey** attended the University of Nebraska. He went into law enforcement and became chief of detectives.
- **Willie Merriweather** attended Purdue University. He became a vice principal and sports agent.
- **Bailey Robertson** attended Indiana Central College. He became a businessman and was involved with the Circle City Classic.
- **Robert Jewell** attended Indiana Central College. He became a biochemist and teacher.
- **Hallie Bryant** played with the Harlem Globetrotters. He became an Army officer, motivational speaker, and businessman.

- **Bill Scott** attended Butler University. He became a teacher, high school coach, and counselor.
- **Joseph King** attended Indiana Central College. He became a businessman and insurance executive.
- **Bill Mason** joined the armed forces. He became a plant supervisor.
- **Winford O'Neal** became a plant supervisor and businessman.
- **Bill Hampton** attended Indiana Central College. He went into law enforcement and became a businessman and insurance executive.
- **Sheddrick Mitchell** attended Butler University. He was involved in postal operations and banking.
- **Henry Robertson** attended the University of Cincinnati. He worked for the Ohio Department of Youth Services.
- **John Gipson** attended Indiana Central College. He became a foundry technician and author.
- **Bill Brown** attended Tennessee State University. He became a fireman.
- **Sam Milton** became a plant operations specialist.
- **John Bridgeforth** attended Indiana State University. He became a foundry supervisor.
- **Stan Patton** attended Tennessee State University. He became an activist and author and worked in business operations.
- **Jim Enoch** attended Clark College. He worked for McDonnell Douglas Aircraft.

- **DeJuan Boyd** attended Butler University. He became a postal worker and building contractor.
- **Charles West** joined the armed forces. He became a captain in the Indianapolis Fire Department.
- **John Davis** joined the armed forces. He became a state of Indiana supervisor.
- **Charles Cook** joined the armed forces. He became a postal worker.
- **Larry O'Bannion** joined the armed forces. He became a brewery specialist in delivery operations.
- **Willie Gardner** joined the armed forces and played professional basketball. He went into law enforcement and became an onsite dispatcher.
- **Benny Cook** joined the armed forces. He became a moving contractor.
- **T. Tolliver** joined the armed forces. He became a postal worker.
- **James Cornett** joined the armed forces and attended Indiana Central College. He went into middle management.
- **Harold Crenshaw** joined the armed forces. He became a banquet set-up specialist.
- **Norman Crowe** joined the armed forces.
- **Herbert Swanigan** became a foundry operations specialist.
- **Levern Benson** attended Miami of Ohio University. He became a department head of personnel.

- **Willie Posley** joined the armed forces. He worked for Bryant Heating.
- **Robert Jones** joined the armed forces. He became a postal worker.
- **Ludwig Johnson** joined the armed forces. He became a computer specialist and businessman and was involved with the Circle City Classic.
- **Willie Burnley** joined the armed forces and attended Central State College.

Indiana Basketball Hall of Famers

The 1955 and 1956 teams were inducted into the Indiana Basketball Hall of Fame in 2005 and 2006, respectively. In addition, twelve individuals who played at Crispus Attucks under Coach Crowe have been named to the Indiana Basketball Hall of Fame since 1982.

- Oscar Robertson (1982)
- Hallie Bryant (1983)
- Willie Gardner (1986)
- Bob Jewell (1988)
- Bailey Robertson (1990)
- Albert Maxey (1992)
- Edgar Searcy (1993)
- Larry McIntire (2007)
- Bill Scott (2012)
- Levern Benson (2013)
- Bill Hampton (2017)

Team Accolades

In addition to the personal accomplishments of the Attucks players, the championship teams have continued to be recognized in many ways over the years.

- In 1980, the 1955 senior team members were named to the Indiana Basketball Hall of Fame Silver Anniversary Team. The Silver Anniversary Team is made up of outstanding senior basketball players on the twenty-fifth anniversary of their graduation.
- In 1981, the 1956 senior team members were named to the Indiana Basketball Hall of Fame Silver Anniversary Team.
- In 2004, the NCAA Hall of Champions in Indianapolis recognized the 1955 team.
- In 2005, the Crispus Attucks Museum recognized the 1955 team on the fiftieth anniversary of their championship win.
- In 2005, the Indianapolis City Council recognized the 1955 team on the fiftieth anniversary of their championship win.
- In 2005, the 1955 team was inducted into the Indiana Basketball Hall of Fame.
- In 2005, the 1955 team was featured in the documentary *Something to Cheer About.*
- In 2006, the 1956 team was inducted into the Indiana Basketball Hall of Fame.
- In 2010, the 1955 championship team was honored at halftime of the NCAA Championship Game in which Duke University defeated Butler University. The game was played in Indianapolis, and Oscar

Robertson, Willie Merriweather, Bill Hampton, and John Gipson attended the ceremony.

- In 2013, the 1955 team and their rival, Gary Roosevelt High School, were honored in a celebration at the Lakeshore Classic tournament. Oscar Robertson from Crispus Attucks and Dick Barnett of Gary Roosevelt were keynote speakers. The event was televised on ESPN.
- In 2013, the 1955 team was honored by the Indiana House of Representatives.
- In 2014, the 1955 team was featured in *Indianapolis Monthly* magazine.
- In 2014, the 1955 team was honored by Butler University in Indianapolis.
- In 2014, the 1955 team was honored by Marian University in Indianapolis.

The 1955 Crispus Attucks championship team were Grand Marshals of the Indianapolis 500 Festival Parade in 2015.

- In 2015, the 1955 team was named Grand Marshals of the Indianapolis 500 Festival Parade in downtown Indianapolis.
- In 2015, IUPUI honored the 1955 team at the christening of a new campus building. The building is located at the site of the Lockefield Gardens Dustbowl.
- In 2015, The Family Inc. honored the 1955 team.
- In 2016, the 1955 team was honored in a documentary by Spike Lee called *Little Joints.*
- In 2016, the 1955 team was honored in a session of Congress by Indiana Senator Dan Coats.
- In 2016, the 1955 team was honored by the Indiana Pacers on the anniversary of the movie *Hoosiers.*
- In 2021, Converse released a shoe commemorating the 1955 team during Black History Month.

Converse Pro Leather High Top
"Crispus Attucks"

Chapter 25: Crispus Attucks Museum

The Indianapolis Public School Board's Multicultural Education Program planned the Crispus Attucks Museum. Its director of the program, Mrs. Pat Payne, manages it. The codirector, Gilbert Taylor, is the museum's curator and a 1955 Attucks graduate. He holds degrees from the University of Indianapolis and has lived and studied in Africa and several European cities. The museum is truly a state-of-the-art facility, and it is one of the top facilities of its kind in the United States.

It houses memorabilia, artifacts, and information of all kinds about Black culture all over the world. It tells of the historical accomplishments by Black people from all walks of life. Education, sports, music, the military, and business are a few that come to mind. The museum houses a gift shop that was set up with the help of the Crispus Attucks Class of 1954. The museum, which is located in the rear of Crispus Attucks Middle School, has meeting rooms, an auditorium for press conferences, general offices, and storage space for film, books, pictures, and other priceless artifacts. It is something people of all races, cultures, and age groups should see.

The museum is connected with the new gymnasium, which holds and displays trophies, team pictures, and memorial tributes to past coaches and also tributes to legendary athletes who played for the high school. The success of the Crispus Attucks basketball program in creating a dynasty unequal to any other sports program in the state of Indiana helped to spur racial harmony statewide.

While many schools already had one or two Blacks on their teams, they started adding more. The old philosophy of a quota of Blacks was dropped. Black students were eventually bussed to schools outside the main Indianapolis central district (IPS), which enabled white schools to get more top-quality Black athletes. The onset of bussing took many of the Black students to schools such as Ben Davis; Southport; Avon; and the many township schools in Decatur, Wayne, Warren, Washington, and Franklin Townships as well as bringing in whites to the inner city schools of IPS, thus changing the complexity of the athletic programs. As a result, Crispus Attucks's enrollment dropped immensely, and eventually, despite protests by the Black public and its civil leaders, the school was closed permanently. Despite this desperate move of the educational administration to integrate the schools, interaction socially and otherwise amongst the Black and white students was not forthcoming.

Members of the 1955 and 1956 basketball teams with the Crispus Attucks museum director.

Standing, left to right: John Clemons, Bill Hampton, Bill Brown, Willie Merriweather, John Gipson, Sam Milton

Seated: Pat Payne

The school was reopened as a middle school a few years later, and it housed the Crispus Attucks High School Museum. The Black public and its leaders' vigorous protests brought this about. The school was also placed on the National Register of Historic Buildings in the United States. Its storied history in education and athletics has been, hopefully, preserved for all times. In 2006, the school changed from a middle school to a magnet high school. It is now home to students from sixth through twelfth grade who wish to pursue careers in medicine.

All the Crispus Attucks players on the 1955 and 1956 championship teams are actively involved to ensure the school's place in history here in Indianapolis and in the state of Indiana's archives. Racism has been eliminated on the playing field, so to speak, but not on the social and business fronts. But things are getting better each decade as time goes on.

I would admonish all young people not to dwell on the past, and despite any obstacles or hindrances they may encounter today, never stop trying and never give up. If one gives their best at all times, the best of things will come eventually. Just learn from the past, appreciate what barriers others have torn down, and live for the future.

Chapter 26: The Ending

After an annalization and brief summary of the trials, tribulations, and setbacks encountered by the Crispus Attucks basketball team, one conclusion comes to mind. This team was one of destiny, carefully picked by a higher power to absorb and deal with the racial prejudices of those times. God gets all the glory. We were blessed to be able to go the entire championship seasons without any major injuries and sustain the camaraderie we had on and off the basketball floor. We had the best coach, who was able to motivate us and sustain the winning attitude necessary for our impending success.

We had great teachers who saw to it that we were students and good citizens first, to precede our status as outstanding basketball players. Several of those teachers were first in their chosen fields, going through the same things we did in their quest to be the best they could be. One person that comes to mind is Mr. Graham Martin, better known as Coach Martin. He was the second Black to play football at Indiana University. He was also one of the first Blacks to attain the rank of captain in the United States Navy. He and twelve other Black men received the rank of captain during the same time. They endured a lot of social injustices during their tour of duty.

We had the best student body following in the state (past graduates included) and the best cheerleaders. They were second to no one. Their singing the "Crazy Song" was truly inspiring.

Last but not least, we had the entire Black community behind us. They listened to the games on the radio if not able to attend. Some came to the games, even driving hundreds of miles to attend road games. Thus, we always had a booster section wherever we played. They used to see us thumbing rides to school and other places and would always stop and offer us a ride. If they thought we were in any impending physical danger, they were right there to make sure we were alright. If we were unknowingly in a dangerous or criminal environment, we were quickly rushed away and chided for being there.

Mr. Albert Booth (deceased), who was working his way up the ranks on the Indianapolis Police Department, was a mentor of sorts for Bill Brown, Patton, Enoch, Sam Milton, and me. He always would take time to tell us of the ramifications of any devious deeds if we became involved. He would preach the value and necessity of getting an education. He made sure we were enlightened on all aspects of the law and why it paid to follow and obey the law. We truly appreciated him.

As was stated previously, all of the prestigious Black social clubs during those times honored us after our championship seasons. They were proud of us and treated us as if we were their own boys. Julius Thomas, my father-in-law, was a member of the Cosmo Knights Social Club, which honored us.

Dr. Charleston B. Cox, who I became good friends with, used to provide us dental service, even if the charges exceeded the amount we had available. He gave me a gold crown that I still have today. He was truly a good friend and mentor.

I remember when I had an outstanding game once out at Indiana Central College, he reminded me to stay grounded and concentrate on academics first. I'll always remember that piece of good advice.

After reminiscing through the entire journey, we all as players appreciate the fans, public, and news media for all of their support, and we give God all the glory.

Special thanks goes out to my sister-in-law, Mrs. Beverly J. Asher, and her husband, Robert M. Asher, who were invaluable in producing this book. No one appreciates this book and its contents more than she does. My wife,

Becky, also gets high accolades for her criticism towards the book's final assembly.

Additionally, *The Indianapolis Recorder*, one of the top Black newspapers in the country, is to be commended for its vast coverage of our games. Jim Cummings provided outstanding commentary, while Jim Burres and Thom Ervin provided photography of all games we played.

Resources

Our thanks go out to the following people for their contributions towards the writing of this book. We are deeply appreciative.

- Joe Buckhalter
- Henry "Cookie" Woods
- Oscar Robertson
- Samuel Hatten
- Sam Milton
- Ray Crowe
- Bill Brown
- Mrs. Willie Gardner
- James Enoch
- Mrs. (Florence) Bill Scott
- Henry Robertson
- Maxine Coleman
- Al Maxey
- Mrs. Betty Crowe
- Norman Crowe
- Milton Baltimore Jr.
- Bill Hampton
- Gilbert Taylor
- Bill Mason

Photo Credits

1. Coach Ray Crowe
   Indianapolis Recorder Collection, Indiana Historical Society

2. Crispus Attucks 1951 Basketball Team
   Muncie Evening Press

3. Oscar Robertson
   Indianapolis Recorder Collection, Indiana Historical Society

4. 1955 Crispus Attucks State Champions
   Indianapolis Recorder Collection, Indiana Historical Society

5. Crispus Attucks High School
   Courtesy of John Gipson

6. Members of the 1955 and 1956 Crispus Attucks Championship Teams
   Indianapolis Star

7. Championship Parade, 1955
   William Palmer/Indianapolis News, Indiana Historical Society

8. 1956 Crispus Attucks State Champions
   Indiana High School Basketball Historical Society

9. John Gipson at Indiana Central College
   Courtesy of John Gipson

10. Bailey Robertson at Indiana Central College
    Indiana Basketball Hall of Fame

11. Hallie Bryant at Indiana University
    Indiana University Archives

12. Prather's Hot Shots, 1963 Lockefield Dustbowl Champions
    Courtesy of John Gipson

13. 1959 Crispus Attucks State Championship Team
    Indianapolis Recorder Collection, Indiana Historical Society

14. Oscar Robertson with Julian Gipson
    Courtesy of John Gipson

15. 1955 Championship Team as Grand Marshals of the 500 Festival Parade
    Courtesy of John Gipson

16. Converse Pro Leather High Top "Crispus Attucks"
    Converse/Culture Kings, https://culturekings.com

17. Members of the 1955 and 1956 Teams with the Crispus Attucks Museum Director
    Courtesy of John Gipson

www.ingramcontent.com/pod-product-compliance
Lightning Source LLC
LaVergne TN
LVHW020047110826
845155LV00029B/668

* 9 7 8 1 9 4 3 4 1 4 3 1 4 *